YOUR KIDS

DR. PAUL R. MARTIN

Zondervan Publishing House
Grand Rapids, Michigan

A Division of Harper Collins *Publishers*

Cult-Proofing Your Kids
Copyright © 1993 by Paul R. Martin, Ph.D.

Requests for information should be addressed to:
Zondervan Publishing House
Grand Rapids, Michigan 49530

Library of Congress Cataloging-in-Publication Data

Martin, Paul R.
   Cult-proofing your kids / Paul R. Martin
     p. cm.
   Includes bibliographical references.
   ISBN 0-310-53761-4 (pbk.)
     1. Cults—United States—Controversial literature. 2. Cults
—United States—Psychology. 3. United States—Religion—1965–
I. Title.
BL2525M365   1993
291.9—dc20   92-35835
                                               CIP

Some of the names in this book have been changed to protect the privacy of the individuals described.

Edited by Leonard G. Goss and Lori J. Walburg
Cover design by Jack Foster

Printed in the United States of America

93 94 95 96 97 98 / DH / 10 9 8 7 6 5 4 3 2 1

CONTENTS

ACKNOWLEDGMENTS

There is an entire cast of players who made this book possible. While I was involved in a cultic "fringe" group, several outside the group sounded the alarm. First, there were John and Ray Williams, who tirelessly warned me of the group's use of authoritarian and ethical excesses. Don Norbie, a Christian author and pastor in Greeley, Colorado, also expressed concern. At the time I did not listen to them. But as I began seriously to question the integrity of the group, I was reminded of their words. Once my own doubts surfaced, I remained silent for months, fearing reprisals if I spoke out. The only exception was the continued talks I had with my wife, Barbara.

One night, Tony Castro, who now teaches at Gordon College, threw out the tiniest hint that he too had questions. For me it was an open door finally to find someone who would listen to and verify that I was not crazy. Soon Scott Jones, now a missionary in Brazil, and I were talking and comparing notes. My confidence grew that indeed I wasn't insane or spiritually unfit. Once we had decided to leave, I prayed to God, and asked him where Barb and I were to go. It was actually during these heart-felt prayers that John White of Geneva College phoned, requesting that we come to Geneva for job interviews. That was the open door. After leaving, Stan and Debbie Berberick were the first ex-members we spoke to. Words can't express how much it meant for someone to listen to me and understand. Many thanks to both of them.

Don Shell and Ray Armstrong, of North Hills Bible Fellowship, listened to me without judging. They put no pressure on me to get "back into the race" prematurely, giving me time to heal.

When I left the group where I was involved, I knew I was free, forgiven, loved, and accepted. The bondage of seven and a half years was finally gone. That experience of grace is still as sweet and fresh. I thank Lt. Col. Ray Moore, Jr. for being the instrument of God to allow me to start helping victims of these experiences. I owe him many thanks for his years of support and encouragement.

My parents, brother, and sister have tirelessly supported Barbara and I in this pioneering work. Their unbelievable dedication is a continuing example and encouragement to me.

Dr. Michael Langone, executive director of the American Family Foundation and Dr. Ron Enroth, of Westmont College, have really understood me. Confronting cults and helping former cultists is a tough, demanding, and lonely business. So few seem to understand. Ron is a pioneer in pointing out that cults and new religions are more than a doctrinal issue. Thanks are due to Mike and Ron for being there and for understanding.

Special thanks goes out to all those who have come to Wellspring Retreat and Resource Center for healing from cult involvement. Their stories have made this book possible.

Larry, our staff counselor, helped me with research and editing and completed the bibliography. This book would not have been finished without his help. Rhoni went the second mile in seeing that the manuscript was typed on time.

6

Acknowledgments

I could write a book of acknowledgment to my wife alone. Barbara always believed in me and supported the decision to leave the group. She has made Wellspring work. Her energy, genius, and devotion make the impossible possible. Many sit in the arena of life watching while a tiny few in the arena are battling for their lives and for the lives of others. Barbara is one of the few. There could be no greater soldier or companion in battle. In the midst of the impossible circumstances of treating an ever rapidly growing number of ex-cultists, running Wellspring, and maintaining a private practice of psychology, she told me I could write this book. She had more faith in me than I did! No other wife has sacrificed so much and loved so much.

PREFACE

Fifteen to twenty years ago I could boast haughtily that I was like David's men, for I thought I, too, understood the times and knew what I should do (1 Chron. 12:32). In my senior year of high school I experienced the shock and horror of losing our president, John F. Kennedy. I still remember the day well. It was a Friday, and in preparation for a big basketball game that weekend the Wheaton Academy pep band was warming up for a pep rally. As the baritone player for the band, I was there wearing my straw hat and my red and white pinstriped shirt. However, we didn't have our rally that day. Instead, a teacher walked in, and with deep sorrow announced the shooting of our president. My youthful idealism began to shatter.

A few years later our generation was into the Vietnam war, the hippie revolution, drugs, sex, and heavy metal rock and roll. "Flower children" were everywhere. My evangelical church seemed cold and uncaring. Idealism was at an all-time low. A few years later, I joined the "Jesus Movement." This was the Christian youth version of being a hippie, or at least of being anti-establishment. My needs for friendship, purpose, and belonging seemed to be met at last.

During that time I read voraciously. I probably read one thousand books. As a Christian I know well the problems of the world. I had read most, if not all, the books of C. S. Lewis, Francis Schaeffer, Jacques Ellul, Os Guinness, Clark H. Pinnock, B. B. Warfield, Hal Lindsey, G. K. Chesterton, John Warwick Montgomery, Friedrich Nietzsche, Karl Marx, and Søren Kierkegaard, along with numerous biblical commentaries, various theological works, some of the church fathers, and much more. I also read books on the cults, such as James Bjornstad's *Counterfeits at Your Door*, Kenneth Boa's *Cults, World Religions, and You*, Pat Means's *The Mystical Maze*, and Jan Karel Van Baalen's *The Chaos of the Cults*, to name just a few. At that time I held the traditional view of what a cult is—any religious body that holds beliefs and practices clearly in opposition to historic Christianity as expressed in the Apostles' Creed.

Ironically, however, I was being swept away by an evangelical Christian movement that was growing more and more cultic itself. In the early seventies the group was known informally as "The Blitz." Later it gave itself the name "Great Commission International" (GCI) and "Great Commission Church." A few of the cultic practices I began to see exercised by GCI in 1977 were the use of deceit, the claim that our group had discovered the only correct way to evangelize the world (a practice that was lost after the first Christian generation and then was rediscovered by the founder of our movement), and the suppression of any sort of questioning or confrontation of the leadership. Nothing I had read prepared me to see the warning signs when I joined.

Ultimately, by 1978 the lack of ethical standards I perceived on the part of GCI's national leader finally woke me up. He was able to justify veiled deception and outright misrepresentation as effective means of getting out the Gospel. To question this was to be divisive. For seven months, I struggled in vain to get this leader to listen. The experience for me and my wife was like being interrogated in a Communist Chinese prison. During that time she suffered a miscarriage, and I was physically, mentally, emotionally, and spiritually exhausted. My father, an evangelical pastor, heard of these discussions and was enraged. Normally a calm man, his anger flared. I will never forget what he said about my leader: "Paul, I have met thousands of people in my life, but when I met your leader, cold chills ran down my spine. He is the most evil man I have met in my life. . . . He is a false teacher . . . he throttled you."

At first I dismissed my dad's words; I was still loyal to my leader, in spite of being rebuffed by him. But because of my dad's concerns, I began to question more things. A few others in the group began to open up. We compared notes. We discovered that we saw the identical problems—the suppression of questioning, inaccurate interpretation of Scripture, and the use of deceit. Because of troubling issues like these, I left GCI in the summer of 1978 to begin a teaching job at Geneva College.

But as I related my story to my Christian brothers and sisters, I could sense that few really understood. Talking about it became painful. I grew embarrassed and withdrawn. The notable exception was the elders at my new church, who listened in quiet support and refrained from offering either quick fixes or judgment.

Later, Barbara and I began to hear of others leaving the group. We heard painful stories of hurt, betrayal, broken health, broken dreams. Often I wept. I still do when I hear of the pain. Those who left became a needed support for each other.

Much prayer and counsel convinced me to switch careers. I wanted to learn more about psychology and religion, in the hope of being able to help others victimized by groups such as Great Commission International.

Barbara and I opened Wellspring Retreat and Resource

Center two years after I received the Ph.D. degree in psychological counseling. To my amazement, I learned that there were innumerable groups around the country like the one we recently left. Hurting people were everywhere. We found it typical that both the ex-cultists and their parents usually had gone through an agonizing search for help. For some, it was years before they found someone to explain the psychological dynamics of cultic mind control phenomena.

As I reflected back on my extensive reading of evangelical Christian literature, I realized that I was *not* one "who understood the times" and knew what he should do (1 Chron. 12:32). I was unprepared to see the dangers of cultism even within evangelical circles.

By "cultism" here I refer not only to doctrinal problems but *behavioral* ones as well. I will examine the tendencies in some groups to "use extreme and unethical techniques of manipulation to recruit and assimilate members and to control members' thoughts, feelings, and behaviors as means of furthering the leader's goals."[1] And when I use the term "evangelical," I refer to the acceptance of various historic Christian doctrines, such as the full authority of the Bible, the triune nature of God, justification by faith alone and not by works, and the necessity for personal spiritual conversion.[2]

Because of my Christian background, I thought I would never join a "cult." But like most evangelicals, I thought of cults as being Mormons, Moonies, the Jehovah's Witnesses, and the usual five-to-ten other groups commonly listed in books written about these movements. Certainly I was not prepared for the dangers of legalism within evangelical ranks. To me, legalism meant all the "don'ts"—negative rules about the use of make-up, about dancing, going to movies, swimming on Sundays, dating, and other trivial things. Little did I know there could be a legalism of "do's"—do read the Bible, share your faith daily, make disciples of others, study the Word, and constantly pray. As good as these things are in themselves, when placed in a context of duty and obligation with the resulting guilt from nonperformance, the "do" version of legalism can be just as deadly as the "don't." One simply never knows how much is enough.

Commitment and dedication were so emphasized in my upbringing that I had absolutely no defenses when challenged by the Great Commission International to be "totally committed to God." No one ever told me that there might be potential dangers where faith commitment is concerned. No one ever warned me of the subtleties of influence factors, and the tremendously powerful techniques used in thought reform. The enemies we were taught to avoid as we grew up were the ones that were blatantly obvious. More "clever" enemies were seldom, if ever, mentioned.

This leads me to a major point. It has become a cliché to say that our world is undergoing great turmoil. Frequently we hear of the "spiritual collapse of the West," and the "moral malaise in our society."[3] Alexander Solzhenitsyn has said that Western civilization should now be called "Western pagan" instead of "Western Christian."[4] He notes the loss of the moral basis of our society.

As evangelicals we are so concerned about the decline of moral values, as well as the rise of secularism and New Age thinking, that few are sounding the alarm about the serious dangers posed by some who actually *champion* moral values, spirituality, and evangelism—yet at the same time advocate cultic behavior. We must see the cult problem within the context of the re-emergence of totalitarianism. Such totalism (the attempt of an autocratic leader or hierarchy to control all aspects of people's lives) is utterly insensitive to boundaries in religion, and this includes the boundaries in evangelical Christianity.

It has been truly sad and horrifying to see the caliber of people coming to Wellspring. Here I see some of the best, brightest, and most attractive youth of our nation. Some were valedictorians of their high schools, most were in the upper ten percent of their graduating class, and many were students at prestigious colleges and universities when they responded to the call of a particular cultic group.[5] They were lured by the challenge of dedication, spirituality, and morality. Now they face months, possibly years, of recovery. Did no one warn them? Did anyone try to prepare them? In their time, Jesus, Paul, Peter, and John all warned about false prophets, false teachers, those who would seek to deceive the very elect. But we are not being similarly warned today.

So I write this book to sound an alarm. Christians have overlooked a great enemy—the enemy disguised as evangelical Christianity. Much of the current harm is done by the most subtle of errors. Great danger threatens the unsuspecting while appearing neutral or even non-religious, and simple Christian faith alone offers little defense against the lure.

If this book can keep even one person—perhaps your child—from joining the sort of group I describe, or speed just one ex-member's recovery, my dreams and prayers will have been answered.

INTRODUCTION

When Richard and Joyce Turner sent their son Michael off to a Christian college, he was bright, handsome, and talented. He often spent his summers at camps, innovative schools, or traveling abroad. One such college-sponsored summer program took him to Chicago. There he was seduced into a cult—the Chicago affiliate of the Boston Church of Christ. At the time Michael reasoned, "My spiritual search is over. I found God."

Shortly after Michael returned home from his Chicago trip, his mother noticed he had changed. Normally a caring, sensitive, and fun-loving young man, Mike was now more serious and judgmental of others. In addition, his relationship with his father dissolved. His life did not seem his own anymore.

For the next year and a half, Joyce and Richard struggled to keep their family together. They asked, "Who were these people that had such a grip on Michael? Is their church a cult? How can we find out?" Joyce, a librarian at a Christian college, was frustrated at every turn. She found, to her horror, that only two libraries in the United States had a copy of Steven Hassan's *Combating Cult Mind Control*, perhaps the definitive book on the psychological aspects of the cult problem.[1] "As a librarian," she told me, "I now know information about cults is terribly lacking."

When she finally found and read some books, she knew there was a problem. Mike had all the signs of a person under the influence of a destructive cult. He was overly serious too much of the time, his sense of humor was curtailed, he had grown detached from his father, and his career and life plans were drastically altered.

Some colleagues who were prominent Christians at her college rebuked Joyce for trying to interfere in her son's life. After all, they reasoned, "It's his life and we don't see anything particularly wrong with the group." Little did they know.

Even though Mike had transferred to another college so he would be close to his newfound group, Richard and Joyce were not going to be stopped in their search for understanding. At Mike's previous college, they found a professor who knew something about the movement their son had joined. Professor Green proved immediately helpful simply by listening to and validating Richard and Joyce's concerns.

Next Joyce called an organization that provided information about cults. Fortunately they had heard of the group Mike was in, and they offered to send her information about it. They gave her some advice on how she and Richard could approach Michael without resorting to the extreme measures of deprogramming—the illegal holding of an unwilling person while others present information that is intended to make the person want to leave the cult.

With the assistance of a skilled professional, Richard and Joyce sat down and shared with Mike their fears, concerns, and all the information they had learned about his church.

At first Michael rebelled. "I don't care what they say," he thought. "I'm not going to leave the group. I'm sure the material they are sharing with me is all wrong. My parents are probably agents of Satan."

Only gradually did Mike begin to see the truth in what his parents and the counselor were saying. He began to see that virtually all aspects of his life were controlled by the group. Spare time, types of entertainment, dating, hours devoted to prayer, Bible study, evangelism, church meetings—all were directed by the church leadership. In addition, he saw that he could no longer justify the Boston movement's purging of negative information about itself. Now he realized that if he remained, he would be supporting something that was wrong. After this, Mike left the cult. However, there were still many issues left unresolved, and it took weeks of intensive daily counseling to help resolve these issues.

Many other families could tell similar stories of trauma resulting from cult involvement. As a result, I write this book for all the parents and children who have suffered, often expending vast amounts of time, energy, and money before finding help. And I write this book as a warning for those parents who have not yet gone through the horrors of losing a son or daughter to a cult. I will share what I have learned and experienced and I will share what I have learned from others, like Richard and Joyce. The purpose of *Cult-Proofing Your Kids* is to offer some guidelines and present some constructive steps to inoculate you and your family against the destructive influences of cults.

THE
CULT
PROBLEM

1
WHAT IS A CULT?

*The path of segregation leads to lynching every time.
The path of anti-Semitism leads to Auschwitz every
time. The path of the cults leads to Jonestowns, and
we watch it at our peril.*
—James and Marcia Rudin, *Prison or Paradise?*
The New Religious Cults

Many Christians think they know all there is to know
about cults. They may reason something along these lines:
"Oh, I've heard about cults; you know, Jonestown, Satanism, and that survivalist group in Montana. You can bet my
kids would never get involved in anything like that. They're
simply too smart—anyway, they're very involved in our
church . . ."

However, most Christians actually know very little
about cults and what makes people join cults. To test your
own general knowledge about cults, take a few minutes to
answer the following true-or-false quiz.

THE CULT SUSCEPTIBILITY QUIZ

1. I am lonely a good part of the time. _____
2. I tend to be a follower more than a leader. _____

3. I am not very satisfied with my church. _____
4. Somehow, I feel my idealism and purpose in life haven't been properly tapped or challenged. _____
5. I've been having some personal problems I can't seem to solve. _____
6. The cult issue is not much of a problem in society. _____
7. There are about ten to twenty cults in the U.S. _____
8. I could spot a cult with little effort. _____
9. Most cultists wear unusual clothing or uniforms. _____
10. Most cults recruit on the street by selling flowers or books, or by requesting a donation. _____
11. There are very few cultic problems within evangelical Christianity. _____
12. All cults teach non-Christian or heretical doctrine. _____
13. I'm not the type of person who joins a cult. _____
14. Most people who join cults are weird. They have "problems." _____
15. Truly dedicated, Spirit-led Christians would never join a cult. _____
16. People are in cults because of spiritual problems. _____
17. People in cults are not "saved." _____
18. Cultism has little to do with totalitarianism or addiction. _____
19. People who join cults know what they are doing. _____
20. Groups that preach the gospel and are winning many to Christ cannot be cultic. _____

If you answered *true* to any of these questions, you may be susceptible to cults. Most people are susceptible to cults either because of unmet needs or ignorance of cult issues. The first five questions on the above quiz suggest that personal unmet needs make a person vulnerable to the right pitch. The remaining fifteen questions reveal typical "myths" and misinformation about the cult problem.

EVERYONE IS SUSCEPTIBLE

Parents may not fully realize the subtlety and deceptiveness of the lure of the cults. But the truth of the matter is, *virtually anyone can get involved in a cult under the right circumstances.* The president of the student body at Wheaton College later became one of Jim Jones' right-hand men. David Berg, a preacher's son who was briefly a Christian and Missionary Alliance pastor, later became one of the most notorious cult leaders in this century. The truth is that smart, well-adjusted kids from good Christian homes can and do join cults.

One reason few recognize their vulnerability to cults is that we fail to understand that our society is faced with a growing and pervasive cult problem. The danger from cults is more insidious than ever as cultic groups become more subtle and skilled in recruiting and retaining members. Many older cults adapt to the times with cosmetic changes designed to make themselves look more acceptable.

THE DEFINITION OF A CULT

Traditionally, cults have been defined as groups that deviate from the orthodox tenets of the Christian faith. For example, Harold Busséll, author of *Unholy Devotion: Why Cults Lure Christians*, states that among other things a cult is "any religious body that holds beliefs and practices clearly in opposition to historic Christianity as expressed in the Apostles' Creed."[1] In his book *The New Cults*, Walter Martin defines a cult as "a group religious in nature which surrounds a leader, or a group which either denies or misinterprets essential biblical doctrines."[2] And Ronald Enroth has aptly commented that "for the Christian, the most significant component of a definition of a cult is theological in nature."[3]

While heresy can and does cause psychological dam-

21

age, orthodoxy does not guarantee that similar psychological and moral injury will not occur.[4] Therefore, a strictly theological definition of the word *cult* is not enough. There also needs to be a psychological definition. Ronald Enroth points out that Christians have neglected the psychological aberrations of cults, and he quotes a concerned Christian layman who said, "I think there is merit for placing more stress on the other danger zones created by cults, such as psychological and moral injury, disruption of family ties, impairment of scholastic and professional careers."[5]

Therefore, many definitions of cults include not only theological, but also psychological elements. Here are a few examples:

> A group that uses methods that deprive individuals of their ability to make a free choice. They use deceitful recruitment techniques, they deceptively and destructively use the devotees' energies, and they capture the devotees' minds.[6]

> Destructive cults are those which tend to use extreme and unethical techniques of manipulation to recruit and assimilate members and to control members' thoughts, feelings, and behavior as a means of furthering the leader's goals. Although most cults that have aroused concern are religious, they can also be political, commercial, or pseudotherapeutic.[7]

> A group or movement exhibiting a great or excessive devotion or dedication to some person, idea, or thing and employing unethically manipulative techniques of persuasion and control (e.g., isolation from former friends and family, debilitation, use of special methods to heighten suggestibility and subservience, powerful group pressures, information management, suspension of individuality or critical judgment, promotion of

total dependency on the group and fear of leaving it, etc.) designed to advance the goals of the group's leaders to the actual or possible detriment of members, their families, or the community.[8]

With these above definitions in mind, another aspect of the cult problem becomes apparent—cults can include groups and organizations that typically are not viewed as cults. These could be fringe churches, psychotherapy groups, New Age organizations, and various extremist political movements.

CULT CATEGORIES

In his book *The Lure of the Cults*, Ronald Enroth categorizes a broad variety of cultlike groups in the following way.[9] (Note: Although the groups catalogued below may exhibit some characteristics of cults, they are not all cultic in the psychological sense, nor are they all necessarily abusive to their adherents.)

Eastern Mystical Groups

These groups consider truth to be far more a matter of personal experience or feeling than of absolute unchanging reality. Most groups in this category can trace their origins to Hinduism, Buddhism, or other Oriental religions that view God, humanity, and the universe as a single reality— in other words, they ultimately subscribe to the religious philosophy of pantheism in one form or another. Included in this category are Hare Krishnas, Zen Buddhists, the Divine Light Mission, the Healthy, Happy, Holy Organization (3HO), Soka Gakkai (or Nichiren Shoshu of America— perhaps the largest and fastest growing cultic group in the U.S.), Ananda Marga, Meher Baba Movement, and Self-Realization Fellowship.

Aberrant Christian Groups

These groups claim to be Christian and Bible-based. Some would argue that they are fundamental and evangelical, but these groups deviate by way of practice and belief from the standards of evangelical Protestant Christianity. Some deviate from historical Christian doctrines that evangelicals and other Christians would consider foundational, but most of their deviations would not be considered actual heresy. This category includes the Family of Love (formerly the Children of God), the Alamo Christian Foundation, the Church of Bible Understanding, The Love Family (or Church of Armageddon), Faith Assembly, the Church of the Living Word ("The Walk"), The Way International, The Christ Family, University Bible Fellowship, the Boston Church of Christ, Maranatha Christian Ministries, and Great Commission International. Even the excesses of the Shepherding Movement, founded by Bob Mumford, Derek Prince, Don Basham, Ern Baxter, and Charles Simpson may be classified as an aberrant Christian group.[10]

Although dozens of additional fellowships could be cited, I have included a broad range of groups so that one may get a fuller sense of the nature of aberrational Christianity. Other aberrational Christian groups or movements—especially some televangelists, some faith-healing ministries, and the "Positive Confession" movement—have been dealt with in recent literature. However, doctrinal deviations evidenced by some televangelists and fringe churches do not necessarily imply they are cultic in the psychological sense. For more information on "fringe" churches, see chapter 2.

Psychospiritual or Self-Improvement Groups

These groups do not normally function as churches or even as religions—i.e., they do not typically have a "house of worship" in anything approaching the traditional sense, nor do they have regularly scheduled meetings for the performance of religious rituals. Rather, they more typically offer workshops, seminars, or personal sessions to teach techniques or provide therapy purportedly to aid in self-improvement, self-discovery, self-actualization, and personal transformation. Services are provided for a price (usually steep) and are based on Eastern-mystical philosophy. Some of these types of groups would include Synanon, the Forum (formerly est), Transcendental Meditation (TM), Lifespring, and Scientology.

Eclectic/Syncretistic Groups

These groups usually combine strands from several religious traditions into a new "hybrid" religion. This is "smorgasbord religion." The Unification Church, for example, is a combination of Eastern philosophy, spiritism, and Christianity. Other groups in this category also usually combine a mix of Oriental religion and traditional Christianity. This category includes, besides the Unification Church (also known as Moonies), the Church Universal and Triumphant (headed by Elizabeth Clare Prophet), Eckankar, Bahá'í, and Sufism.

Psychic/Occult/Astral Groups

These groups feast on "secret" wisdom and knowledge supposedly once held by a few ancient seers. It is usually claimed that this secret wisdom was lost with the rise of science and technology. The resulting void has caused some to search for these "lost truths." Although most of these "lost truths" originate in the Eastern religions, a fair share of them come from spiritism, paganism, and witchcraft. The Aetheris Society, along with various other UFO Cults, the Association for Research and Enlightenment (founded by Edgar Cayce), and Astrology are included here.

The Established Cults

These are large religious movements that in most cases arose in the nineteenth century as religions that deviated in some significant way from the teachings and practices of traditional orthodox Christianity. These are groups or churches which claim to be based on the Bible in whole or in part, and yet deny or distort core doctrines of the Bible, such as salvation by faith in Christ alone apart from legalistic works, the Trinity, the deity of Christ, the inspiration and authority of the Bible, the person and deity of the Holy Spirit, etc.—doctrines which the Christian church throughout its history has consistently affirmed. This heading would include the Church of Jesus Christ of Latter-Day Saints (the Mormons), Christian Science, Jehovah's Witnesses, Unity School of Christianity, and others.

Extremist Political/Social Movements

These are movements that can be cultic in the psychological or social sense but are not necessarily religious in nature. They can resort to violence, intrigue, deceit, and terror to achieve their ends. As a rule these movements feel that the existing authorities must be dealt with by any means necessary to remove them from power. In addition, their goals are primarily political as opposed to religious, though they often espouse a twisted version of Christianity. Groups such as the Aryan Nations, Posse Comitatus, the Ku Klux Klan (KKK), the White Aryan Resistance, Lyndon LaRouche's political movement, and certain extremist terrorist movements represent this kind of cult.

THE PROLIFERATION OF CULTS

Current estimates of cult membership in America range anywhere from around two million to over twenty million. In addition, there are probably at *least* two million former members of cultic groups (according to cult expert Louis J. West). Further, the late Walter Martin, a premier resource on cults, noted that eighty percent were once members of Christian churches! The typical estimate for the number of different cults in America ranges from two to five thousand.[11]

Twenty years ago, few had heard of groups like the People's Temple, the Family of Love, the Hare Krishnas, Silva Mind Control, est, Nichiren Shoshu of America (Soka Gakkai), Self-Realization Fellowship, or a plethora of other cults and new religious movements. Many of those groups were so small at that time that few even sensed their dangers. Most of the new religions have sprung up in the last twenty-five years.

The above estimates of the number of cults and cultists are undoubtedly conservative. Many groups are quite small—anywhere from four to several hundred members—and usually they do not attract extensive research, study, and publication. For example, the "no-name" cult led by Jeffrey Lundgren in Kirtland, Ohio, would never have attracted national attention were it not for the 1989 murder of a family of five who belonged to this small sect, a split-off of the Reorganized Church of Jesus Christ of Latter-Day Saints. It would have remained, like so many others, virtually unknown, uncharted, and ignored.

These unidentified fringe and cultic groups pose three serious problems. First, they cloud the issue about *what is* and *what is not* a cult. Usually only the larger or more established groups, like the Mormons, Jehovah's Witnesses, and the Unification Church, to name a few, are included in books dealing with cults. Readers often get the erroneous impression that if a group in question is not listed in the book, then it must not be cultic.

Second, the size of many of these smaller groups means they are relatively obscure, making it very difficult to estimate accurately the true number of cults or their members. There simply are too few researchers to identify and study all of these small and sometimes obscure groups. However, a number of nationally known cult-watch groups do analyze and record the groups that come to their attention. But even these professionally-staffed organizations cannot keep up with all the new groups, nor, because of limited resources, have they published information on all the ones they *do* know of.

Third, lack of information on these small groups places a greater burden on parents, educators, pastors, and counselors to determine whether the groups are simply "different" or in fact destructive. Consequently, some self-education and research are a must.

EVALUATING A GROUP

If you want to find out whether a certain group is a cult, ask yourself three questions. First, does this group deviate from orthodox Christianity; that is, are they cultic in the *doctrinal* sense? Second, does this group practice such things as coercion; that is, are they cultic in the *psychological* sense? Third, do they believe strange or esoteric things or engage in unusual or bizarre practices; that is, are they cultic in that they deviate from socially accepted norms? If the answer to any of the three questions is yes, the chances are you are dealing with a cult.

To help you clarify your thinking, I have provided the following chart. Take a moment and identify what category your particular group falls into (established cult, aberrant

Christian, etc.). Then try to answer the three questions. If you find that you do not know enough about the group to complete the checklist, chapter 13 will give you some specific guidelines on how you can find out more information about a group.

Type of Group	Heretical *Doctrinal deviance* [yes, no, not sure, not applicable]	Coercive *Behavioral deviance* [yes, no, not sure, not applicable]	**Bizarre? Non-conventional?** *Social deviance* [yes, no, not sure, not applicable]
Eastern mystical			
Aberrant Christian			
Psychospiritual or self-improvement			
Eclectic/syncretistic groups			
Psychic/occult astral groups			
The established cults			
Extremist political/ social movements			

2
FRINGE CHURCHES

Unlike physical abuse that often results in bruised bodies, spiritual and pastoral abuse leaves scars on the psyche and soul.
— Ronald Enroth, *Churches That Abuse*

A. W. Tozer once said that sin can thrive at the very altar of God. And the sin of cultism thrives within the ranks of orthodoxy. Because aberrant Christian churches— or "fringe" churches, as they are sometimes called—are such a large problem, I have chosen to cover them in a separate chapter.

Only God knows the untold numbers who have been spiritually damaged by those who subscribe to all the fundamentals of the faith. But many well-known church leaders refuse to hear complaints of hurting Christians who report deceit and hurt brought to them while under the pastoral care of other Christian ministries. These complaints are far too often summarily dismissed because "They preach the gospel," or "God is blessing their ministry," or "Look at the fruit they are producing."

However, pastors and parents alike need to look beneath the cloak of orthodoxy and examine the actual behavior, conduct, and activities of a particular church or ministry, as well as how they influence the lives of members. Because our definition of cults includes those groups that psychologically manipulate their members, there are some theologically orthodox churches that may actually be cultlike in their practices.

CHARACTERISTICS OF FRINGE CHURCHES

Ronald Enroth, professor of sociology at Westmont College and author of *Churches That Abuse,* has written extensively on the fringe group problem.[1] These "fringe" churches are generally orthodox in terms of doctrine, but they possess other characteristics that set them apart from mainstream evangelicalism, including:

1. *Control-oriented leadership.* A great emphasis is placed on submission and obedience to group authority.

2. *Spiritual elitism.* A "we" vs. "they" mentality. These groups view themselves as either the only "true Christians," or as the only ones who really have the current "vision."

3. *Manipulation of members* (environmentally and informationally). Members are frequently told where to live or work, who to date, what to read, and even where to go for their vacations.

4. *"Siege mentality" and perceived persecution.* Any criticism is viewed as "persecution"—others seem to be out to get them.

5. *Lifestyle rigidity.* Strictures are often enforced regarding sleeping, eating, exercise, and leisure time.

6. *Emphasis on the subjective experience.* Undue stress on "words from the Lord," "God showed me," "the Lord told me," and "I sense the Spirit."

7. *Denunciation of other churches.* Those outside are viewed as "lukewarm," not "spirit-filled," "dead," lacking vision or dedication, and lost.

8. *Suppression of dissent.* Criticism is viewed as faction, slander, rebelliousness, and evidence that one is lacking a teachable spirit.

9. *Harsh discipline of members.* Those who question teachings or practices of the group are often shunned and their reputations ruined by public exposure of their "sin."

10. *Painful exit process.* Target members may be cut off without warning—this may include loss of financial support if employment is within the group; formerly close friends will break all ties.[2]

WELL-KNOWN FRINGE CHURCHES

Ron Enroth hears about new "fringe" churches almost on a weekly basis. We at Wellspring also get letters and phone calls constantly from concerned parents all over the country describing some new fringe churches in which their children have become involved.

Although information on new fringe churches is sadly lacking, here is an overview of the more well-known fringe groups. Judging from their statements of faith, one could consider these churches clearly Christian. But they have been accused by numerous former members and outside observers of manipulative techniques and authoritarian control.

Faith Assembly

This fundamentalist fringe group was founded by Hobart Freeman, a former professor at Grace Theological Seminary and author of a popular textbook in Old Testament published by Moody Press. Freeman taught that divine healing extended to shunning all doctors, rejecting health insurance, and facing ridicule from the world and fellow Christians. Members were threatened with excommunication for disobedience. Over eighty children of parents who were part of Faith Assembly died as a result of their parents' failure to give them medical attention.

Maranatha Christian Fellowship/Campus Ministries

This authoritarian charismatic group was founded by Bob Weiner. In Maranatha, there were rules for nearly every aspect of one's life, including what types of material one could read, who to date, whether to have health insurance, who to marry, and when to visit parents. Excommunications and shunnings were at times very painful to those cast aside. Often the reasons for the discipline had more to do with violation of the group's extra-biblical rules than anything having to do with correct doctrine or morality.

"The Walk" or Church of the Living Word

On the surface, this church seems like a typical charismatic group. It was founded by John Robert Stevens, however, who taught a version of the notion that men can become God, that his teaching constitutes the only true church, and that he and other ministers of the church can engage in sexual immorality with some of the female members. The intensity and demands of belonging to The Walk has resulted in psychological distress to some of the members. In at least one case, it led to the suicide of a prominent member.

Community Chapel and Bible Training Center

Founded by Donald Barnett of Seattle, Washington, this pentecostal church encouraged "dancing in the spirit" between "spiritual connections," or members of the opposite sex not married to each other. This is a practice that Barnett claimed was revealed to him by an angel of God. In many instances this practice led to sexual immorality, the breakup of marriages, the split of the church, and a number of lawsuits. In addition, Barnett, who was dismissed from the church in 1989, has been described as highly authoritarian; his word could not be challenged by his members without some adverse consequence.

Greater Grace World Outreach (formerly called "The Bible Speaks")

Started by Carl Stevens in Maine, the headquarters of the Greater Grace World Outreach was later moved to Lenox, Massachusetts, where the group flourished despite allegations of immorality and money mismanagement, and the loss of a huge law suit. In this suit, Betsy Dayton Dovydenas, whose father was one of the original founders of the successful Dayton/Hudson Retail Corporation, alleged that Carl Stevens used undue influence to elicit a "donation" of nearly seven million dollars from her. The courts eventually agreed, ordering a refund of $6.5 million and forcing the church into bankruptcy. Unable to repay such a large sum, Stevens was compelled to turn the church's Lenox compound over to Dovydenas and then to relocate in the Baltimore area. Yet, recently there appeared an advertisement in *Christianity Today* magazine for Carl Stevens's latest book, and a picture of Stevens standing next to the president of the National Religious Broadcasters appeared in another Christian periodical. Stevens continues to broadcast a radio program in the Baltimore area, as well as to advertise his non-accredited Bible School.

The Alamo Christian Foundation

Tony Alamo started this foundation during the heyday of the Jesus Movement in the sixties. No doubt many were genuinely converted to Christ through the early days of the ministry. But the inner surface of the group today reveals followers reduced to virtual slavery. The wrath of God features far more prominently than God's love in the teaching of the leaders, and this is evident in the very atmosphere in the group itself. Disciples who leave the group are viewed as forever lost. Tony Alamo himself spent two years trying to raise his deceased wife, Susan, from the dead—through his and his followers' prayers. To this date the coffin containing her body is missing. Reportedly, Alamo's group broke open her mausoleum and spirited the coffin away in order to prevent her body from falling into the hands of federal marshals about to take possession of the cult's compound in Arkansas. Alamo faces several legal charges and was a fugitive from justice from 1988 until captured by the FBI on July 5, 1991. Today, this cult operates churches in California, Illinois, Tennessee, Arkansas, and New York. All but one use other names and make no reference to Alamo or to the Foundation. Few would suspect that the Holiness Tabernacle Church of Dyer, Arkansas, for example, is an Alamo Church.

The Potter's House/Victory Chapel/The Door

This is a Pentecostalist sect that generally holds to traditional Pentecostal theology. Many have claimed that the sect's views on healing and tongues are unbiblical and harmful. For example, miracles and healings are *expected* to occur—if they don't, the believer is left crushed, feeling he or she lacks sufficient faith. Other serious concerns are the leadership's heavy-handed authoritarian nature, the excessive amount of activity and requirements demanded of the members, and the uniformly negative reports of former members who claim they were under mind control.

University Bible Fellowship

This group actively recruits on college campuses, never telling potential recruits anything of the intense demands that will be required of them should they join. The group is very authoritarian, and it views other churches as dead and uncommitted to Christ. Confession of sins to leaders is a central hallmark of UBF church practice. Originating in Korea, this confession ritual is called a "sogam." These sogams are often written and rewritten, until the leadership feels they capture the thrust of the individual's sins. Allegations of the group's use of mind control are frequent among former members with whom I have spoken.

Multiplying Ministries/
The Boston Church of Christ Movement

This movement was originally called the Crossroads Movement, having begun in Gainesville, Florida, by Chuck Lucas. Lucas was then the evangelist of the Crossroads Church of Christ in that city. A disciple of Lucas's, Kip McKean, is now the chief leader of the Boston movement. He is based at the Los Angeles Church of Christ after moving there from Boston. Having been the center of authority in Multiplying Ministries for so long, "Boston" eventually lent its name to the movement. There are now "pillar" churches and "daughter" churches all over the world.

The Boston movement is growing rapidly, and has

caused considerable controversy in many locations. The campus chapters of the movement have run into a great deal of difficulty with university officials and have been expelled from a number of campuses, including Vanderbilt University, the University of California at San Diego, and Washington University in St. Louis, to name but a few. The group's chief emphasis is on discipleship, that is, a process of extremely close supervision and the personal instruction of every member. Each new member is assigned a "discipleship partner," and each older member is expected to make disciples of new members. The entire structure is organized into a pyramid system, where eventually everyone is accountable to the one at the top, namely Kip McKean. Perhaps the most damaging of the group's practices is that of confession of one's sins to the discipling partner. Often the discipler may extract confessions from the disciple, thus inducing a type of guilt or shame. "Reconstruction" is a process that all disciples must go through to prepare for baptism, but only after the follower is *totally* repentant. The extent of this reconstruction process goes well beyond the bounds of confession of one's sins to God, or even to the one who has been sinned against. Many feel guilty for being who they are; their personality becomes their sin. For example, introverts are often made to feel that introversion is a sin that must be repented of. This process has actually led a few of those active in the movement to commit suicide, suffer mental collapse and clinical depression, and has led in some cases to psychiatric hospitalization. I personally have treated dozens of ex-members who have suffered from the rigors of this terrible discipling process. Much has been written about the Boston Movement. Currently it is the largest fringe aberrational cultic movement active in this country. It is very successful in recruiting some of the most talented college students in our nation. Children raised in evangelical Christian homes and others who have a personal faith in Christ are not immune to this group. The leaders in the Boston Movement are highly trained, well-organized, and can conduct very effective church services.

Great Commission Association of Churches (formerly known as Great Commission International and originally called "The Blitz Movement")

Great Commission started during the Jesus Movement in the late 1960s and early 1970s, and from there it grew rapidly. Within a few years there were over five thousand followers with chapters on nearly every major university campus in the Midwest and the South. Local chapters had names like "Iowa State University Bible Studies" "the Cornerstone," "the Solid Rock Fellowship," and "New Life." Its chief distinctive was the notion that God had given us the "Vision," a divinely inspired "strategy" based on Acts 1:8 to reach the world for Christ in this generation. ("But you will receive power when the Holy Spirit comes on you; and you will be my witnesses in Jerusalem, and in all Judea and Samaria, and to the ends of the earth.") When I was a member of GCI during the 1970s, our leaders maintained that no other group had this same "vision," and critics were expelled for questioning or challenging this vision of the leadership. GCI was highly authoritarian, and demanded strict commitment from all followers. Many ex-members have faced long years of therapy trying to recover from their experience in this group. Some have attempted suicide. Still others, some ten years later, sustained such psychological damage that they have been unable to get on with their lives, often taking jobs well below their educational and intellectual qualifications.

Some encouraging reforms have occurred in recent years after the founder, Jim McCotter, left the movement in the late 1980s. However, the current leadership has not yet revoked the excommunication of its earlier critics. The admissions of error so far have been mainly confined to a position paper, the circulation of which has been questioned by many ex-members. Furthermore, Great Commission leaders have not yet contacted a number of former members who feel wronged and who have personally sought reconciliation. There has been some positive movement in that direction, but most ex-members that I have talked to are not fully satisfied with the reforms or apologies and feel that the issues of deep personal hurt and offense have not been adequately addressed.

Sword of the Spirit

This is the largest Catholic charismatic movement in the United States. Recently several of the leaders of the Word of God community in Ann Arbor, Michigan (the leading community in the movement), including co-founder Ralph Martin, have admitted that the organization had indeed been guilty of many authoritarian excesses and had even practiced mind control techniques. Similar admissions of abuse occurred in the SOS-related Catholic charismatic communities in Steubenville, Ohio, and Pittsburgh, Pennsylvania. Bishop Albert Ottenweiler has been assigned to make recommendations on correcting the excesses and developing a program of recovery.

Parkview Community Church of Arcadia, California

Founded by John Gattuso, Parkview is a "mildly charismatic" fellowship that has had historic ties to the evangelical community. In the past Gattuso was a frequent speaker for Campus Crusade for Christ, and many current members of his church were once staff members of that organization. Gattuso is also a psychologist who has conducted therapy with female members of his congregation, aiding them in getting rid of their "sexual idolatry." Part of this process has reportedly involved nudity, oral sex, and, at times, sexual intercourse. The licensing Board of the State of California revoked his license to practice psychological counseling. Nevertheless, Gattuso continues as pastor of the Parkview Church and many of his members remain committed to him and are undaunted by the criticism. While some members support Gattuso's views on sexuality, some parents of former members have expressed outrage at Campus Crusade for being silent for so long about Gattuso's practices.

Many other fringe churches exist beyond those mentioned. Most fringe groups are small, and there exists no clear body of research from which to learn about them. This is why it is important to learn to evaluate these other groups by doing the basic research yourself. You are the best person to cult-proof the ones you love.

3
WHY DO PEOPLE
JOIN CULTS?

What prepared men for totalitarian domination in the non-totalitarian world is the fact that loneliness, once a borderline experience usually suffered in certain marginal social conditions like old age, has become an everyday experience of the evergrowing masses of our century.

—Hannah Arendt, *The Origins of Totalitarianism*

Why do people join cults? Doctrinal issues alone—such things as the nature of God, the Trinity, the inspiration of Scripture, the return of Christ, the person and work of Christ, and the incarnation, important as they are—have little, if anything, to do with why most young people join cults. The three main reasons why people join are: (1) healing for emotional hurts, (2) establishing friendships and relationships, and (3) spiritual growth.

HEALING FOR EMOTIONAL HURTS

Early childhood experience usually contributes to the emotional needs that one exhibits as an adult. The unmet emotional needs of a child from a broken, cold, or abusive home may make a cult seem more attractive. "Here," the person may reason, "is the love, the warmth, and the security that I never had as a child." He or she may think, "I've found my true family." The person enmeshed in the cult may often in fact start to call the leaders of the group "Mom" and "Dad."

Others are attracted to cults because they offer help with personal or drug problems. Sad to say, in these cults the members often feel more loved, cared for, and secure than in more traditional churches. They enjoy teaching, often-wanted and needed discipline, and a strong prayer life. And they learn how to help and express love to others.

Research shows that young people are more vulnerable to cultic affiliation during or immediately after suffering a severe crisis. Some of these crises are the death of a relative or close friend; a broken romance or a divorce in the family; job loss or inability to find employment; poor grades or failure in school; excessive amounts of business-related travel for one or both parents; illness, whether of self or a close friend or relative; transition from high school to college; or, criminal victimization, including burglary, rape, or mugging.[1]

Why are kids more vulnerable during or after one of these crises? It is because each one of these situations represents a loss—and introduces both a lack of control and feelings of helplessness. We all need certain things to live life normally, including friends, a job, a sense of being accepted by our peers, a feeling of self-worth, and an absence of trauma.

Most cults train their recruiters to minister to felt needs. Susan, a college student, had recently lost a close friend and had performed poorly on exams. Susan mentioned the loss of her friend to Leann, a casual acquaintance. Leann, a fringe church member and active recruiter, carefully and sensitively responded to Susan. They got into a conversation. Leann listened attentively, and occasionally uttered such remarks as, "Oh, that must be a terrible loss for you," or "You seem sad and feel that no one understands." Finally, she offered to talk with Susan again, then she invited her to a meeting.

People in cults or fringe churches are good listeners. This casual friend allowed Susan to open up about her personal troubles. During a crisis situation, Susan was not concerned with *why* someone would care so much about her problems, or why a casual acquaintance would seem a bit too caring.

Jehovah Witnesses actually recruit some members by reading and following up on the obituary columns, because they know people are vulnerable after the loss of a spouse, a relative, or a close friend. One of my good friends, Don, lost his mother to the Jehovah's Witnesses after his father died. In the first few weeks after his death, friends, relatives, and members of their church were supportive—they sent cards and flowers, and made frequent visits with words of support. People dropped off meals and offered to run errands. But after the first several weeks the pastor, the church members, and the friends erroneously assumed the crisis was over. They went back to their normal affairs and left the grieving widow alone. But the Watchtower cult didn't; they continued to support Don's mother. She was lonely and grieving, and they were there for her.

This woman had been active in the church all her life, and she prayed and read her Bible daily. She took pains to see that her three sons were raised in the church and were active as Christians. Nevertheless, she joined the Jehovah's Witnesses. Why? Simply because this group gave her the continued love, support, friendship, and understanding that she needed during a crisis. Actually, people need the most support *after* the two-to-three weeks of a severe crisis or loss. The cults have learned that when most people stop calling and showing care, that that is the time to begin. *They* did it and the *church* didn't. She is still a member of the Watchtower society, viewing the church she once faithfully attended and served as an apostate group falsely worshipping Jehovah.

ESTABLISHING FRIENDSHIPS AND RELATIONSHIPS

Young people also join cults for friendships and relationships. Parents need to keep in mind that cults are usually better at showing attention, concern, and love than the average religious organization. Part of cult-proofing your kids is to forewarn them that any group or person seeming to be too loving, too caring, and overly-concerned must be responded to with extreme caution.

According to Harold Busséll, cultic recruits were attracted by "group sharing, community and caring."[2] In my own work with former cult members I can certainly concur. One young college man I counseled was attracted to a cult because of the warm "relationships" between people. A young woman who attended one of the Big Eight universities told me she joined a fringe church because they spent time with her, teaching her how to become a Christian. A young man from the east coast joined a well-known cult, The Way International, because he "made a lot of friends in the group." And a woman from Pennsylvania with a degree from the University of Michigan joined a hyper-charismatic fringe church because of the "fellowship." She also said that the "relationships were phenomenal" in this group.

For more information on the characteristics of friendships in cults, see chapter 10.

SPIRITUAL GROWTH

The third reason people join is spiritual. Many honestly want to know and serve God, and the vitality of evangelically-minded groups attracts them. A young man who came to me for advice claimed his "relationship with God" had grown as a result of his involvement in a cult. An Ivy League graduate told me that what attracted him was the group's "zealous Christianity." A young woman from New England with a graduate degree joined a campus fringe church because it appeared to her "more biblical" than the church in which she was raised.

Three things should be kept in mind here. First, we each have a spiritual need that beckons us to begin a quest. Second, a person's search or spiritual quest may be intensified when he or she has had *inadequate* religious training and nurturing. And third, the spiritual quest may also be intensified when a person has been *adequately* nurtured by a *sound* church!

I am continually surprised by the spiritual hunger I see in the young people at Wellspring. So many who were burned in cult involvement started out with a sincere and praiseworthy desire to serve God. Yet it was the cult or fringe church that offered a vital solution to their quest, and not the church, which was often viewed as impotent and bland by comparison.

We all have spiritual needs. These needs may be intensified by a deficient religious upbringing. I do not suggest that only children from such backgrounds will enter cults or fringe churches, or that parents should feel guilty for whatever inadequacies existed in the religious training given to their kids. A number of studies have shown that the type of childhood religious training does not necessarily determine who will eventually join cults or abusive organizations. Rather than feel guilty, parents should consider how they may better facilitate the spiritual needs of their children, communicating with them and offering sound spiritual alternatives.

In fact, people young and old join cults not only because of a weak religious background but also because of a *strong* one. Many join because they have come from active, vital churches, and they often see a "fringe Christian" group as a further step to a vibrant and dynamic Christian life. For example, a solid evangelical Baptist becomes a leader in the Children of God. Or, a graduate of an evangelical college, and a dedicated Christian, joins the Mormon Church. Or, three seminary graduates from solid evangelical divinity schools wind up in a "fringe church," where they are burned, betrayed, and used.[3]

Why do genuine, dedicated Christians join cults or fringe Christian churches? The reason is that we all desire "something more." Our dedicated youth do not often see the cult's level of zeal and dedication in their own churches. The siren song of a cult or a fringe group beckons them. All too often we confuse vitality and charisma for truth and soundness.

4

MYTHS OF
CULT INVOLVEMENT

*The great masses of people more easily fall victim to a
big lie than to a little one.*

—Hitler, *Mein Kampf*

As I have said, evangelicals typically view the cult
problem from a theological vantage point. This means that
not only are the psychological aspects often overlooked, but
also that a number of myths have arisen regarding the
psychological consequences of the cultic movement. Here
are six of these myths.

> **Myth #1: Ex-cult members do not have psychological
> problems. Their problems are wholly spir-
> itual.**

Although this is often believed by both Christians and
ex-cultists, this myth has little basis in reality. As a result
of extensive research with some three thousand former cult
members, clinical psychologist Margaret Singer of the
Berkeley campus of the University of California observed
significant instances of depression, loneliness, anxiety, low

self-esteem, overdependence, confusion, inability to concentrate, somatic (bodily) complaints, and, at times, psychosis.[1]

My own experience verifies Singer's findings. Lori, a young woman I treated after she left an aberrational church group, was overdependent and insecure. She asked me: "Is it okay to have cold cereal for breakfast?" "Can I listen to the radio?" It was as though Lori were a little child needing approval and guidance for her every move.

Spiritual problems are often present *in addition* to the emotional distress. These spiritual problems, however, generally originate with a cult's unbiblical teachings and practices rather than with an individual's own relationship with God. Almost all former members of religious cults or extremist sects (including those which are doctrinally evangelical[2]) are confused about such things as the grace of God, the character of God, submission to authority, and self-denial. It is noteworthy that groups with widely varying doctrinal stances—from the Hare Krishnas to Jehovah's Witnesses—uniformly distort God's grace and character.

> ### Myth #2: Ex-cult members *do* have psychological disorders. But these people come from clearly "non-Christian" cults.

This myth assumes one of two things. First, it wrongly assumes that genuine Christians never have psychological problems. However, as Francis Schaeffer wrote:

All men since the fall have had some psychological problems. It is utter nonsense, a romanticism that has nothing to do with biblical Christianity, to say that a Christian never has psychological problems. All men have psychological problems. They differ in degree, and they differ in kind, but since the fall all men have more or less a problem psychologically. And dealing with this, too, is part of the present aspect of the Gospel and of the finished work of Christ on Calvary's cross.[3]

Second, this myth wrongly assumes that there are only non-Christian cults. Yet some Christian groups are in fact cultic in *practice*, believing that they have an exclusive corner on a particular biblical truth, or that, while there are other Christians outside the group, theirs is the only one that has God's fullest blessing. Many, if not most, of these groups usually require unquestioning obedience to their leader in virtually every detail of life. This being the case, abusive Christian groups can and frequently do cause psychological problems.[4]

A number of recent studies has shown that psychological distresses are experienced both by members in Bible-based (and even doctrinally orthodox[5]) groups and by non-Bible-based groups.[6] The psychological problems are in fact quite similar. Flavil R. Yeakley, Jr., reports that a certain type of group-induced personality distortion has contributed to guilt, low self-esteem, frustration, depression, serious emotional problems, overdependence, and irrational behaviors in a number of well-known religious organizations.[7]

Maranatha and the Boston Church of Christ essentially are evangelical Bible-based ministries. Maranatha is a fundamental, charismatic sect advocating "dominion theology" or "kingdom theology"[8] that has been criticized frequently for authoritarian excesses, among other things. In November 1989, the senior leadership of Maranatha, including founder Bob Weiner, dissolved the corporate organizational structure of the network of Maranatha churches (though leaving intact the campus ministries) following admissions of authoritarian excess, including requiring members to obtain permission for such things as going home for the weekend, telling members what type of job to take, whether to purchase health insurance, and who to marry.[9] Likewise, the Boston Church of Christ and its many sister churches all over the United States and abroad have been roundly criticized for authoritarianism and coercive persuasion techniques. Yet both of these groups would probably contain a majority of "born-again" members.

What is alarming about these findings is that groups like these, which are at the very least marginally Christian, are producing psychological harm quite similar to that produced by out-and-out non-Bible-based cults. All of these groups were molding their members into a composite personality that included extroversion and judging (essentially relating to the world in terms of value judgments). But not all people are by nature extroverts or judger-type personalities. Some are by nature introverts and perceiver-types (those who view the world in a more descriptive manner without needing to draw conclusions based on their observations). Attempting to alter personality types invites disaster in the form of neurosis (nervous disorders without discernible physical foundations) and other emotional difficulties.

Yeakley also tested members of the mainline Churches of Christ (distinct from the Boston Church of Christ) as well as members of Catholic, Baptist, Lutheran, Methodist, and Presbyterian churches. In these mainline groups he did not find *any* evidence of group-induced personality distortion that would lead to psychological distress.

Still, orthodoxy by itself is no absolute guarantee that psychological or other harm will not occur. My own research (with several hundred ex-cultists and over 200 on an intensive basis—totaling at least three thousand hours) indicates that the severity of problems suffered by those in the more extremist evangelical sects may be equal to or, in some cases, greater than problems experienced by members of the better-known cults such as the Hare Krishnas, certain eastern groups, the "Moonies," various New Age cults, or The Way.[10]

> **Myth #3:** **Both Christian and non-Christian groups can produce problems, but all of the people involved in the groups must have had prior psychological hang-ups that would have surfaced regardless of what group they joined.**

I encounter this myth regularly among both Christian and secular psychologists. It seems that no amount of contradictory evidence can persuade some that "normal" people can get involved in cultic groups. Sometimes I try reminding my colleagues about Nazi Germany to help to dispel this myth from their thinking. I ask, "Were all those Germans suffering from individual pathologies that made them vulnerable to the Nazi religion?" Or I might ask, "How about Iran and the Ayatollah Khomeini? Are all of his followers fanatical, or were they fairly normal people who became fanatical *because* of following him?"

Some clinical research shows that only a minority of cult members had prior psychological problems before getting involved in cults or extremist religions. In fact, the proportion of those *with prior problems* (about one third) to those *without* is only slightly above the general population (about one fourth). Researchers Saul Levine, Neil Maron, John Clark, and Lorna and William Goldberg have all shown in separate studies that family or other pre-existing psychological factors cannot be used to predict who will join a cult.[11] Further, their findings are consistent with the dynamics of large social movements—such as the Nazis, the fanatical Muslims, or Communism. Simply put, individual psychopathology does not adequately explain the phenomenon of large, fanatical mass movements.

We simply do not know all the factors about who joins cults and why. Nonetheless, there are a few variables that *do* help in predicting who will join a cult. Those variables include: (1) a stressful event within the previous year; (2) a transition phase in life, such as a phase between school and career, or between dating relationships; (3) a longing for community and caring friends; and (4) a desire to serve a great cause and be part of a movement that will change society.

For those who *do* have pre-existing problems, cultic life can be extremely dangerous. They may suffer from detachment from reality, inability to think or concentrate, psychosis, hallucinations, anxiety, depression, or extreme suggestibility.[12]

> **Myth #4: While normal non-Christians may get involved with cults, born-again evangelical Christians will not. Even if they did, their involvement would not affect them quite so negatively.**

This is perhaps the most dangerous myth of all because it blocks the way for any real help. However, even God's sheep can be abused by wicked shepherds (Ezek. 34:1–8). On this passage St. Augustine wrote:

> The defects of the sheep are widespread. There are very few healthy and sound sheep. . . . But the wicked shepherds do not spare such sheep. It is not enough that they neglect those that are ill and weak, those that go astray and are lost. They even try, so far as it is in their power, to kill the strong and healthy.[13]

It bears repeating. Evangelicals and other Christians are not immune from cults. And certainly we should recognize that our children are also at great risk and very vulnerable.

Randy, an evangelical Christian at a major midwestern university, wanted to find a campus fellowship that was "on fire for the Lord." After finding the "perfect church," Randy was quite happy and content—for a time. Then he fell in love with one of the young women in the church. However, the church frowned on dating. Before Randy knew it, his casual and circumspect encounters with this woman, viewed by the elders as disobedience and faction, resulted in his excommunication. Randy respected the elders, so much so that he accepted as true their charges that he was wicked. Although he tried to make amends with the church, he was never able to satisfy the elders.

The experience so stunned Randy that he never regained his former spirit of contentment. For ten years he remained an outcast, even believing he was an outcast from God. Any attempt to work or return to school was short-lived. He was haunted by feelings of rejection. In desperation, his parents sought many forms of help. Some of the finest psychiatrists in the country found it difficult to reverse the damage done. Now a middle-aged man, Randy still struggles with confusion, despair, occupational uncertainty, and difficulties relating to women. Even though Randy was a Christian in a so-called Christian church, he displayed the same symptoms of disillusionment, depression, confusion, and despair as many young people who have been influenced by more well-known cults.[14]

God's sheep *can* be damaged by bad shepherds, and no more obvious examples of "wicked shepherds" could be given than the leaders of destructive cults and aberrational religious movements.

The fourth myth is particularly dangerous to the

Christian community because it ignores the fact that a sizable portion of those involved in cults or extremist groups come from some type of evangelical church base.[15] Of the clients I have worked with personally, approximately twenty-five percent of those involved with cults come from evangelical or fundamental churches, and over forty percent have backgrounds in the large, more historic liberal Protestant denominations.

> **Myth #5: Christians can and do get involved in these aberrational groups and they can get hurt emotionally, but all they really need is some good Bible teaching and a warm, caring Christian fellowship. Then they will be fine.**

Many Christian young people join groups after the group passes a quick test for doctrinal purity. But true "doctrinal soundness" isn't the exclusive elixir for recovery. In fact, most people don't join for doctrinal reasons. Rather, they want to do something exciting for God, and they want to see their efforts in life make some difference. Sadly, they may look at their own churches and not see much happening, so they go to the fringe churches where there are signs of vitality, growth, and vision.

Still, many believe that good Bible teaching and caring Christian fellowship will prove to be the final cure-all for recovering cultists. However, even correct Bible teaching and caring Christian fellowship will not enable all former cult members to recover completely. Many suffer new rounds of spiritual disillusionment.

This myth is false because many persons who have left these groups *do not want* Bible teaching or Christian fellowship. They are "once burned, twice shy."

According to a recently published survey of about three hundred ex-cultists by Flo Conway and Jim Siegelman, the following essentially *nonreligious* activities proved to be very important for rehabilitation of the ex-cultists studied:

- love and support of parents and family members – 64%
- insight and support of former cult members – 59%
- professional mental health counseling – 14%
- acting to recover lost money, possessions, etc. – 9%
- going back to school or college – 25%
- finding a job and establishing a new career – 36%
- helping others emerge or recover from cults – 39%
- establishing new friends unrelated to cults – 50%
- getting as far away from cults as possible – 29%[16]

Although many ex-members of the extremist Christian groups do return to evangelical churches, they often continue to suffer. These members typically will seek a church that is very similar to the one they left. Such people leave their former group because they are incapable of submitting to its demands, but they still believe many of its tenets.

For these people life can be an actual nightmare—they feel they have left "the apple of God's eye" because they were, in their own reasoning, "too fleshly" or "too worldly" to keep up the pace. The rigors of cultic life produced in them all the symptoms of *burnout*—a state of spiritual, mental, emotional, and physical exhaustion. Yet in their own minds the world is explained so totally in theological terms that they cannot even conceive of any such term as burnout. Instead, they wrongly conclude that they were not spiritual enough, and that because of their lack of spirituality, they failed, and God has somehow rejected them.

I seldom see these people; usually friends tell me about them. Though these ex-cultists are too ashamed to return to the cultic group, fearing they would only fail again, they continue to believe the cultic worldview and do not seek spiritual or psychological help. Sometimes they involve themselves in a local church only in the hopes of replacing what they lost by leaving the cult. These people need help.

Still others who have left often find it hard to tie in with other congregations. They want to be involved with new groups, have new friends, and contribute to a new religious organization. Yet they often complain about feelings of being controlled, or being told what to do all the time. "I don't know if I can trust church leaders again." "I'm afraid that if I open myself up I'll be rejected again."

Perhaps the majority of ex-members of extremist groups who want to go on with their Christian lives are unable to read parts of the Bible anymore without eliciting negative associations. Verses such as "He who comes after me must first of all deny himself" now have strong negative associations for the ex-member. Scriptural exhortations to "forget what lies behind," or "be teachable" produce understandable confusion and resentment. A phrase like "the Lord would have you do this" may provoke in an ex-cultist strong feelings of disgust, incredulity, anger, or fear. Too many negative memories are triggered by these phrases. Not surprisingly, for these people evangelical fellowship is not a cure-all. Clearly, something more is needed.

Another problem with thinking that good Bible teaching will cure an ex-cultist is that former members of cults or fringe churches have been conditioned to dismiss or subtly redefine certain biblical thoughts that contradict the dogmas of their particular group. Cult members learn to stop their thoughts and to redefine words and processes. Therefore they may think that a Bible study would be dangerous to their faith. Many ex-cultists admit they required a professionally supervised and non-coercive form of "exit counseling" before Bible study was thought beneficial.

Similarly, the cult could have used Bible verses to accuse them of faction and slander—again, with thought-stopping effects. This prevents hurting Christians from hearing and accepting healing Bible teaching and counsel that would free them from the guilt-inducing teachings of the aberrant group. Christians should not overlook or misunderstand the erroneous teachings that serve as subtle control mechanisms. In certain fringe Christian groups, control mechanisms are frequently contained in their teachings on faction, slander, submission, or confession.[17]

It is necessary, then, for us to be familiar with a particular group's teaching on these subjects. This will allow ex-members an opportunity to open up their minds and entertain thoughts that may have been previously viewed as "slander"—but now can be viewed as "sound doctrine" or even "reproof." I cannot underscore too much the importance of getting these ex-members to *think*, and to think critically.

> **Myth #6: Perhaps the best way for former cult members to receive help is to seek professional therapy with a psychologist, psychiatrist, or other mental health counselor.**

As with the previous myth, this myth is only *half* true. It is therefore also particularly dangerous. Professional therapy is helpful—*but only if the therapist has some expertise regarding cultic phenomena.* Unfortunately, therapists have been known to fail miserably if they are not sensitive to the issues of cult involvement.

For example, in their ignorance some therapists downplay the damaging effects of cults.[18] Other uninformed therapists may unconsciously subscribe to myth #3, and those who do may inadvertently play the "blame the victim" game, or what social psychologists call the "attribution error" (that the problem lies within the person rather than within the group).[19] Such therapy actually is no therapy and unfortunately can make the ex-member even worse.

Worst of all are the professional therapists who consider not only cultic involvement but also religious interest more generally to be mentally unhealthy. Their approach is to help the ex-cultists look at life more "realistically." Sometimes they are even explicitly hostile toward Christianity. For example, Nathaniel Brandon declares that the Christian beliefs on sin and self-sacrifice are "as monstrous an injustice, as profound a perversion of morality as the human mind can conceive."[20] He encourages counselors to help their clients get free of such destructive views.[21] Psychotherapist Albert Ellis considers the concept of sin as the direct and indirect cause of virtually all neurotic disturbances.[22] Obviously, sending an ex-cultist to therapy subscribing to such views will have a potentially disastrous effect. Counseling from such religiously antagonistic therapists could create a double sense of loss, first from the cultic group itself, and second from overall religious faith. The resulting confusion and spiritual disillusionment could last for years, and this does not even take into consideration the potentially eternal consequences of such "counseling" for the soul.

5
SPOTTING A CULT

*If someone you meet . . . sounds or looks "too good"
or "too smooth" to you or you find yourself becoming
spellbound by their words . . . step back and take
another look. You may be dealing with a psychopath.*
—Walter Schreibman, in *High Risk:
Children Without Conscience*

As a child, Jane attended a Hebrew school, where she
learned all about cults. She was taught how cults recruit
new members: by "love bombing," by offering free meals,
by "weekend retreats," and by using front organizations
that pose as some youth service ministry. She also learned
about specific cults, like the Moonies, the Scientologists,
and the Children of God.

Jane felt prepared for an encounter with a cult. In fact,
she had actually received one of the *best* cult prevention
programs available to anyone in a school setting. Yet all
Jane's cult education was to no avail, for she joined the
Church Universal and Triumphant after having been recruited by a close friend. Later she realized her mistake and
came to Wellspring to recover from her involvement with
this cult.

How could Jane, of all people, find herself in a cult? This young woman did not realize that cults recruit in a variety of ways. Nor did she realize that even the best books on cults leave out hundreds, if not thousands, of other groups that are cultic in nature. Instead, Jane reasoned, "If it isn't a Moonie, or a Way member, or a Scientologist, then I'm not being 'love bombed.' I'm not being pressured to attend any special meetings, so it must not be a cult."

SURFACE APPEARANCES

No one has ever shopped around to join a cult. No one has ever deliberately sought out an organization where they could be manipulated economically, physically, and emotionally. Yet each day, people are lured into cults and fringe groups that promise one thing and deliver another.

How, then, can you spot a cult? How can you get past the initial or surface appearances presented by cults to find out about their inner mechanisms? One way is to recognize the chief characteristics of cults.

CULTIC CHARACTERISTICS

Cults Manipulate People

The key to all recruitment by any cult lies in how they manipulate people. Take a look at these definitions of manipulators:

- Manipulators exploit and/or control themselves as things in self-defeating ways.[1]
- Manipulators "attempt to get someone else to provide for [them] what [they] refuse to provide for [themselves]."[2]
- Manipulators "cannot and will not be happy, ever, even if you sacrifice your mind, heart, and body for

them because they will always be left with an empty lonely person inside themselves."[3]

- The hallmark of the manipulator is to be demanding rather than being aware:
  - The aggressive manipulator *demands*
  - The loving manipulator *cajoles*
  - The weakling manipulator *needs*
  - The strong manipulator *overpowers*[4]
- Manipulators are "numb automatons, wasting hours trying to recapture the past or ensure the future. They talk about their feelings but are rarely in vital contact with them."[5]
- Manipulators habitually conceal and "camouflage real feeling behind a repertoire of behaviors that run the scale from servile flattery to arrogant hostility to withdrawn snobbishness in the continuous campaign to serve his or her own wishes or unconscious needs."[6]
- Manipulators don't allow you to confront them with your true ideas or emotions. Manipulators cannot let you get mad at them, nor can they let you "get inside" them, close to any of their true, though hidden, emotions.
- Manipulators "fear vulnerability, fear being exposed or judged. They are afraid that sustained contact with another will reveal a dimension of themselves that they have so far denied or refuse to see . . . the manipulator chooses to avoid risk by attempting to control those around him or her."[7]
- Manipulators tend to want to control everything, including the conversations of other people. "They evaluate rather than appreciate [. . . they] try to convince others, rather than exchange ideas with others. They limit themselves to safe 'small talk.'"[8]
- Past events—real or imagined—give manipulators

excuses for failure. Many manipulators base their promises on the future. Present-oriented manipulators "talk a lot about what they are doing and may seem to be busy, but in fact they seldom accomplish much of anything."[9]

In order to be manipulated, one must surrender control to a degree. How does this happen? First, manipulators appeal to one's needs, wants, desires, and weaknesses. They offer something that seems to satisfy.

Second, manipulators base their appeal more on emotion than logic. People today seem to be more persuaded by the dynamics of delivery rather than the content of a message. Harold Busséll noted that students at Gordon College were more enamored by a powerful delivery than by the content of a chapel speaker's message. Students almost invariably requested certain chapel speakers be invited back if they were dynamic speakers.[10] Content or substance had little to do with their requests. Unless we become more interested in logic than in emotion, we will be manipulated endlessly by the "package" of the message.

Third, manipulators have learned how to operate as successfully in destructive cults as in consumer fraud scams. Cultists operate like the slick used-car salesman. Snake oil potions of old have been repackaged into the new elixirs of spiritual vitality and physical well-being. Throughout history humankind has fallen prey to easy answers, quick fixes, and great bargains.

Cults Do Not Allow Questioning

True leadership allows questions, and even recognizes the importance of disputes on occasion. One of the prime hallmarks of cults or other groups with cultic tendencies is the condemning of questioning.

A friend commented recently on how upset she was on

seeing a bumper sticker that read "Question Authority." Like so many other evangelicals, she saw questioning authority as a sign of anarchy, disrespect, and rebellion. However, the Bible not only permits the questioning of authority, but it also says it is every Christian's *responsibility* to question authority. For example:

- Paul chides the believers in Colosse for *not* questioning their leaders. He writes, "See to it that no one takes you captive through hollow and deceptive philosophy, which depends on human tradition and the basic principles of this world rather than on Christ" (Col. 2:8). He adds, "Therefore do not let anyone judge you by what you eat or drink, or with regard to a religious festival, a New Moon celebration or a Sabbath day" (Col. 2:16). He tells the Colossians, "Do not let anyone who delights in false humility and the worship of angels disqualify you for the prize" (Col. 2:18).

- The Bereans were commended because they didn't just blindly accept Paul's interpretation of the Scriptures. As Luke put it, "Now the Bereans were of more noble character than the Thessalonians, for they received the message with great eagerness and examined the Scriptures every day to see if what Paul said was true" (Acts 17:11).

In contrast to this spirit, cultism thrives in the belief that questioning authority is sin. But questions can represent a legitimately inquisitive and analytical mind. If only the people had been allowed to question Jim Jones long before they drank the poisoned beverage. It is not questioning itself that reflects rebellion, as almost all cultists teach, but the *attitude* of the questioner that may indicate defiance of authority.

Cults Require Submission to Authority

Cults demand dependency and call it biblical submission. In reaction to this false concept of submission, people throw out the concept of true submission altogether—because it is wrongly viewed as unhealthy, crippling, and psychologically enslaving. Sadly, that is what many *do* experience when they subscribe to the *cultic* type of submission—unhealthy, crippling, psychological dependency.

In cultic submission, there is little or no opportunity for self expression. Assertiveness, initiative, questioning, and expressing feelings of individuality are strictly forbidden or severely discouraged. In cultic submission, people fear rejection, crave approval, need constant reassurance and advice from their leaders, and panic when they fear they have displeased them.

Cult "submission" is dependency—not submission. What is healthy submission? In biblical submission there is no denial of one's personality, thoughts, feelings, or expressions. To "deny self" does not mean to deny one's personhood. We are to deny the selfish, sinful, hurtful qualities of the self, but certainly not our personhood. We submit because we want to serve another person, or facilitate a certain ministry. After all, Christ was in submission to his disciples—he served them constantly.

Paul, an apostle who submitted to the Lord and to the brethren, did not hesitate to confront Peter for his hypocrisy in refusing to eat with the Gentiles (Gal. 2:11–14). Neither did godly women of Scripture hesitate speaking their minds when the situation required. Caleb's daughter requested that she receive an inheritance not only of land, but of springs as well (Josh. 15:19). Sarah protested the continued presence of Hagar and her son. This was not being unsubmissive, because God told Abraham that he should listen to Sarah and send Hagar and the boy away (Gen. 21:8–21). Abigail completely overrode her husband Nabal, after he refused to offer food and supplies to David's army, by providing the necessary provisions to David's men. This prevented David from taking mortal vengeance against Nabal. David thanked God for Abigail's generosity, and praised her wisdom (1 Sam. 25:9–38).

In biblical submission, we may have to give of our time, talents, and energy to please and serve others, but not to our own detriment. I submit to my employer in performing my job as instructed. But I will not submit to attempts to label me and define my existence. I will not allow anyone to tell me what I should or should not feel. I obey when asked to do something in line with my job responsibilities, but I am not obligated to submit to that which is wrong.

As a faithful Christian and a serious church member, there are times when I voluntarily submit. However, the authority of church leaders lies mainly in the area of faith and morals. Beyond the responsibility of instruction concerning correct doctrine and the promotion of moral behavior, church leaders cannot rightfully expect submission. Even in these areas, leaders have no authority to go beyond the clear teaching of Scripture. There are *many* secondary points of doctrine in which the church has always been undecided (the method of baptism, the role of women in the church and the home, the form of worship, etc.). On such points pastors and others are free to give their opinions and conclusions, but apart from clear and unambiguous Scriptural teaching, no one has the authority to compel acceptance of their personal views.

This applies also to matters of behavior or lifestyle. When the Scripture is silent, leaders may not legislate. They may direct members to biblical principles, and suggest ways to apply these principles to specific situations, but they must leave the final decision as a matter between an individual and God. In the second chapter of Colossians, Paul clearly teaches that Christians should not obey their leaders on matters unrelated to the Gospel, or on things that are actually a distortion of the Gospel itself. In that context, the prescription to observe certain days, to eat or to abstain from certain foods, or to take special note of leaders boasting of visions or delighting in certain types of self-abasement was to be avoided. Paul's implication for us is clear—honoring leaders has its limits, and the responsibility for discerning truth is never taken away from the individual Christian. We are to evaluate all things in the light of what we know to be truth—the Gospel as originally taught by the apostles and as we find it in the New Testament.

Nor am I obligated to submit by remaining silent if my pastor sins. Paul tells us in the first chapter of Galatians *never* to submit to anyone who teaches or practices error. Paul himself refused to sit by while so-called spiritual leaders behaved hypocritically (Gal. 2:11–14). In fact, a true sign of my submission to my pastor will be that I *do* confront him or her when they are wrong, and continue to follow correct biblical guidelines in confronting him until there is a change in behavior.

One last word about submission. The entire concept of submission must be understood in the context of Christian grace and freedom. If submission to another does not result in increased grace and freedom, then it is not biblical submission. It is dependency and tyranny.

Cults Motivate Through Fear and Guilt

Why do we obey another? Is it because we feel compelled, anxious, and fearful? If so, we are headed for trouble. Others can then motivate us by playing on our neuroses—our anxieties, fears, and compulsions.

Cults demand obedience and motivate their victims by using fear and guilt. In fact, some cults and fringe churches frequently teach that if members disobey and leave the group they will go to hell. In some groups disobedient members are publicly ridiculed, and at times even publicly beaten. Sometimes leaders teach that certain curses, diseases, or possibly demonic possession awaits those not fully compliant with the program of the church.

One young man was told after he left his fringe Pentecostal church that his negative influence would bring demonic attacks on his family. Facing an impossible dilemma—not wanting to return to the group's aberrant teaching but not wanting demonic attacks on his family— he chose to kill himself, thinking that at least his family would be spared the demonic onslaught. Driving deep into the woods, he parked his car and hiked into the remotest corners of the forest. There he sat beside a tree and swallowed an entire bottle of sedatives. Fortunately, he was rescued by a woodcutter who found him before it was too late.

This young man's story is not unique. Suicide attempts occur on a fairly regular basis in the cults. Even among those who have not contemplated suicide, I have yet to meet a single person who left a cultic group who denied that the group ruled through intimidation with fear and guilt.

In the first "honeymoon" phase of cultic involvement, members usually put in long and rigorous hours doing whatever the leader tells them is God's will. Many of them work very hard and accomplish many things. In some groups, it may be evangelism. Members may start evangelizing early in the morning and work until long after dark doing things like passing out tracts, knocking on doors, selling literature, or striking up conversations with people in the park. Communalistic "back-to-nature" groups may have their members spend long hours gardening, selling organic foods, or repairing farm equipment. Full-time students who are active in the Boston Church of Christ movement, for example, typically average twenty to thirty-five hours per week in Bible study, Bible talks (evangelistic Bible studies), prayer, evangelism, and meeting with their senior partner who trains them. It is common in a great many cults for male members to be pressed into service as "volunteer" maintenance workers, lawn care workers, chauffeurs, or anything else that is needed for the group leaders. Female members often serve as unpaid baby-sitters, housekeepers, or cooks for the wives of the leadership.

No one should doubt that these groups generate a lot of "fruit" in the areas of numerical growth and financial gain. But what type of fruit is that? Is it genuine, or is it coerced out of fear and guilt? How long will such fruit last? Many members leave these groups because they feel they have failed; they can't stand the pace any longer. They are spent, exhausted, confused, discouraged, and guilt-ridden. Still others turn bitter. A former member of Great Commission International told me that because of spiritual burnout due to his activity with GCI, he will not even set foot in a church. Burnout, fear, and guilt can wreck lives.

Fear and guilt are negative emotions. They can produce tremendous (but temporary) results for religious organizations by way of adding new members, encouraging long hours of work for the "cause," and increasing the wealth and power of the group. Motivation by fear and guilt can solve problems quickly. But they should never be motivations to complete a task and accomplish a mission.

Of course, fear and guilt are neither good nor evil in and of themselves. They are feelings that cannot be denied. But we can't live on them. Fear and guilt are like flashing red lights telling us that something is wrong. The lights say there is trouble, so find the problem and fix it.

Cults Are Fanatical

Although most Christians would at times be tempted to lie, cheat, steal, or commit immorality, perhaps most who are so tempted would not yield. Yet many of these same people who would not yield to carnal temptation could be pushed to other extremes—to devote long hours to a cause, weaken their ties to friends and families, or develop an elitist mentality whereby they view their group as more spiritual or more favored by God than other groups. What they don't realize is that pharisaical fanaticism and extremism are as destructive as the sins of the flesh.

When I belonged to the Great Commission International, a man whom I will call John was also involved. John became one of the leaders of our movement. In the early days, some of the leaders and I had observed some problems with the movement, and we would talk openly and freely to John about these problems. While John agreed with our analysis, he rationalized the team's problems away. He said that we were young and still learning, that there was no spiritual "action" anywhere else, and that nobody else was doing what we were doing to reach the world. Every other group seemed dead by comparison.

In this way, John and countless others excuse excesses and errors of many kinds. And they were often justified by means of Scripture taken out of context. "Be as shrewd as snakes and as innocent as doves" (Matt. 10:16) and "wisdom is proved right by her actions" (Matt. 11:19) were two of the most abused verses.

Other groups have protected their pastors from charges of immorality with similar reasoning. "How could such a dynamic and spiritual soul-winner possibly be wrong?" I know of pastors that justify their own sexual immorality because they "are not like other men," and that "God knows my special needs." Some claim their sexual liaisons are the only way they can show the love of God to some of the women (or in some cases, men). This is how cults and fringe churches justify their practices and excuse their leaders.

Cults Misuse the Holy Spirit

Many spiritual "gimmicks" masquerade as signs of the Holy Spirit. Former child evangelist Marjoe Gortner could "slay" others in the Spirit and perform "healings," and then get people to "speak in tongues"—and this was long after he threw out his Christian beliefs. Often hailed as the world's youngest ordained preacher, he grew increasingly disenchanted with the preaching gig and quit at age thirteen. Some fourteen years later he wanted to expose other evangelists and healers as charlatans and showmen. Gortner cooperated in the production of the movie *Marjoe*, depicting the fraud and slick showmanship many preachers use to convince the flock that the power of the Holy Spirit is moving in their particular service.

Franz Anton Mesmer (1734–1815), the great hypnotist-scientist, could duplicate almost anything seen in a modern day charismatic service. Claiming that he could cure people with magnets, he "cured" a number of hysterical patients who suffered from neuralgia and various other ailments, such as convulsions. His theory of "animal magnetism" was that magnets could transfer certain fluids from the atmosphere to the body, thus rejuvenating it. He was unanimously rejected by the scientific community. It was later learned that his procedures were based on the principles of hypnosis. Thus, the word *mesmerized* now refers to one being hypnotized or spellbound. One of

Mesmer's tricks was to lay a rod on the shoulder of people who sought a cure. Immediately, these people would fall backward, having lapsed into an unconscious state. Mesmer's procedure appears identical to the modern-day healer or evangelist who, placing a hand on the forehead of someone coming forward for prayer and healing, causes the person to lose consciousness and fall backwards, "slain" in the Spirit. Mesmer was doing this long before the modern-day charismatic movement began in the early 1900s.

Some non-Christian religions also practice speaking in tongues, healing, and "spiritual dancing." Many consider these practices problematic for Christians because they can be so easily imitated by those who are not Christians. On the other hand, saying a thing is of the devil doesn't make it so. But the point is that almost all of these phenomena represent altered states of consciousness that can be induced by a variety of means, including deep relaxation, mixed messages which produce confusion or divided attention, heightened emotional arousal, and physical fatigue.

The biblical admonition to "test the spirits to see whether they are from God" (1 John 4:1) still applies. We must exercise extreme caution should our child or loved one join a group where "supernatural signs" are present. Does the church claim that such signs are unique to them? Are the signs accompanied by sound doctrine? Who are the people performing these miraculous signs? Are the healings open to medical verification? Does the pastor forbid others to question his authority or power? If so, the group is probably cultic.

Cults Stress Experience over Reason

Do we *know* the truth because we experience something? No. We know the truth only after we examine the evidence, weigh it, ask questions, look for contradictions, and then make an informed commitment.

Followers of Guru Maharaj Ji, the leader of the Hindu cult called the Divine Light Mission, "knew" he was the truth because they tasted "divine nectar," saw a "divine light," and heard "divine music" after they followed some of his meditation practices. Another example of "knowing" by experiencing would be the devotees of Jim Jones, who were convinced of his legitimacy because of his "healings," his "words of knowledge," and his apparent compassion for the poor.

And Christians can make the same mistake. In the midst of a public discussion on a university campus on the resurrection of Christ, a pastor rose to address the audience and, he thought, to settle the issue once and for all. He said, "I know Jesus lives and that he arose from the dead, because he lives within my heart." He was repeating the phrase from the old hymn "He Lives," but almost everyone cringed at the totally subjective and anti-intellectual nature of this pastor's "faith."

Cults Discourage Individual Freedom

Much of the concept of freedom as we know it today originated from the Judeo-Christian tradition, as many authors have pointed out.[11] The Westminster Confession clearly states the principle of liberty: "God alone is lord of the conscience, and hath left it free from the doctrines and commandments of men . . . and an absolute and blind obedience, is to destroy liberty of conscience, and reason also."[12]

Freedom implies loyalty to truth, to conscience, and to the ability to make one's own decisions about matters of faith, ethics, and morality. Cult leaders, however, claim that their members are not equipped to make wise personal decisions. They attempt to dictate the members' use of time, dating lives, thoughts, and beliefs, among other things.

The lack of freedom lies at the core of cultism. In fact, it is the breeding ground for cultism.

Cults Offer Things That Are Too Good to Be True

Our nation has many programs to prevent consumer fraud and protect our money, yet there are no programs to prevent someone stealing our mental health or our very souls. Unscrupulous business people selling a defective product or service cannot hide behind the first amendment. But religious cults can and constantly do. When the abusive work of destructive religious cults is exposed, the cry often is, "Religious discrimination!"

Whenever anyone offers you a product or service, you should always ask yourself if this sounds too good to be true. If it does, then it probably *is* too good to be true. As Jeannie Mills, a defector from Jim Jones's People's Temple who was subsequently murdered, said:

> When you meet the friendliest people you have ever known, who introduce you to the most loving group of people you have ever encountered, and you find the leader to be the most inspired, caring, compassionate and understanding person you have ever met, and then you learn that the cause of the group is something you never dared hope could be accomplished, and all of this sounds too good to be true—it probably is too good to be true! Don't give up your education, your hopes and ambitions to follow a rainbow.[13]

ASK QUESTIONS!

My wife and I once wrote our friend to warn her that in our opinion her church group had cultic tendencies.

What did she do? She invited the pastors of the church over for dinner and then asked them if their group was a cult! What do you think they told her? "Yes, we are a cult, and we intend to harm you"? Of course not. Manipulative leaders of fringe or cultic churches will never admit that they use guilt, fear, and intimidation to control their members.

Our friend should have asked others. If you are buying a used car, it would no doubt be wise to ask someone other than the dealer about the condition of the car. Take it to a trusted mechanic for a check. Ask your bank how much the car is worth. Just so, if you are unsure of a church group, either one you are about to join or one in which you are currently involved, by all means ask questions! Only by asking questions will you be able to identify whether or not a group is a cult.

Following is a list of questions you may ask about a group. Take the time to answer as many of them as possible. They will help you identify the problem areas in the group and enable you to spot a group with cult-like tendencies.

- What is so appealing about what the group offers?
- Does the group make its members feel good, fearful, guilty, or a combination of those feelings?
- Does the group leader have a special charm and persuasion that its people find inexplicable and hard to resist?
- Do the people in the group seem a bit too friendly, loving, smiling, and happy?
- Do the people in the group visit or call and offer to help with almost anything?
- Does the group claim to have a special mission or calling that is unique and not found elsewhere?
- Does the leader claim to have unique powers, vision, knowledge, or other abilities?

- How many leaders have left the group, and for what reasons?
- What is the group's reputation in the community?
- What legal actions have been taken against them?
- Are there any checks and balances to the leadership and power structure?
- Does the group have a constitution or laws of government?
- How many meetings does the group have each week? Are the meetings always required?
- Do the people talk about their pastor all the time, as though he were next to God?
- What is the group's view on leadership authority and discipleship?
- What is the group's view on dating and marriage?
- Does the pastor encourage the flock to read different Christian authors, or attend seminars and conferences sponsored by other churches and organizations?
- Is there an isolationistic or elitist mentality?
- If the group is independent or non-denominational, to what associations does it belong?
- Check with other local pastors or civic leaders. Have they heard any complaints about the group?
- Check with selected religious or secular organizations (some listed in this chapter and in other parts of this book) that keep an eye on such groups. Do they know this group? Have they heard any complaints?
- Is the group affiliated with a larger, well-known, and reputable organization?
- What are the credentials of the leader?
- How do your parents, other relations, or close friends feel about the group? Do they have reservations?

- Is the church rabidly separatist?
- What are the finances of the group? Is there secrecy? Does the leader live differently from the followers, drive a better car, take longer vacations, live in a nicer house than people of comparable education and experience?
- Does the group motivate its members mostly through fear and guilt?
- Who invited you to the group or to the meeting? Was it a total stranger? (If so, be *very* cautious.)
- Have any articles been written about the group? Any books?
- Do you know of any criminal investigations regarding the church or its leader?
- Was there a split in the group? Why did it split?
- Are there disgruntled former members?
- Do the disgruntled former members all more or less tell a similar story of why they left? Did they leave because they disagreed with either the teachings or the practices of the group or its leader? How was the disagreement handled?
- Does your "gut-level" feeling about this group tell you from time to time that something is wrong?

We must ask and we must teach our children to ask such questions if we are going to cult-proof them in our society.

TEACHING
AND
PARENTING
CULT-FREE
KIDS

6

THE HEALTHY FAMILY

The proper time to influence the character of a child is about a hundred years before he is born.
—Dean Inge in *High Risk: Children Without Conscience*

Over the last twelve years I have observed well over one hundred families who have lost one or more of their members to a cult or fringe church. Can I now predict what type of family is more likely to have a member join a cult? Not really. Cult members come from all types of family backgrounds.

The first people I worked with were married. The husband, Dennis, came from a good Christian home. His family was well-educated, and his father taught school. Dennis was recruited while attending an evangelical Christian college. His wife, Linda, was from a well-respected family in her own community. Her father had a doctoral degree; her mother seemed to be a bit on the emotional side, but she functioned well. Neither family could be described as seriously dysfunctional or "troubled."

The second person I treated also came from a "normal" family. The father was a prominent civic leader and a recipient of several awards for community leadership and services. He owned a large and successful retail business. The mother was also active in her community and very involved in her children's lives. This family could not be described in any reasonable manner as being disturbed. There was no divorce, separation, drug or alcohol abuse, no fighting or verbal abuse, or signs of work addiction.

The parade of families over the years runs the gamut. Many cult members *do* come from disturbed or dysfunctional homes, where there has been divorce, or alcoholism, or worse. Yet, often this is not the case. A simple carpenter's family that is warm and caring lost their son to a cult. Another family that was nurturing and sensitive saw their beautiful daughter recruited into a harmful group. A father of high government ranking in another country learned that his son joined a cult while attending college in Canada. An extremely prominent family from the midwest sent their son to Wellspring.

In our ministry at Wellspring we have worked with many families that lost members to a cult. Our experience, along with published research, shows the following broad characteristics about families of cultists:

- Some studies show that the proportion of families that are in some way dysfunctional seems to be higher in cultists' families than in the general population. Such families may be less expressive emotionally and more critical of one another, and often one parent is overcontrolling.[1]
- Other studies show that families with members who have joined cults do not differ appreciably from families with *no* cult members.[2]
- Children in cults are more likely to have had prior "psychological difficulties and problems." However, the proportion of troubled youth is only slightly above the national norms.[3]

- For those joining cults, "religious solutions for life's difficulties seemed to be a viable option."[4]
- The majority of those joining cults have typically experienced a major stressful event in the previous year.[5]

What does this information on families of cultists mean? The findings certainly don't allow us to predict who will join a cult. Those who align with alternative religious groups come from a wide variety of backgrounds and exhibit a wide range of psychological health. The findings also challenge some of the myths surrounding cultism that are so common in our society today (see chapter 4). We tend to want to blame victims for their plight. We want to see victims as less deserving, less healthy, and less intelligent than we view ourselves. We are frankly uncomfortable with accepting cult victims as "people like us." We too often live with the myth that cultic involvement could never happen to anyone in our family. But it can, and often it does, unless we care enough to cult-proof our kids and other loved ones.

All parents need to be prepared, and they can be best prepared if they focus on the following areas:

- Giving children proper religious training
- Improving family communication and dynamics
- Supporting their children during a crisis
- Increasing their knowledge of cults

In this chapter, we will focus on the importance of good communications within the family for cult-proofing children.

THE IMPORTANCE OF COMMUNICATION

Donald Sloat has written two excellent books with the titles *The Dangers of Growing Up in a Christian Home* and *Growing up Holy and Wholly.*[6] In the second book, Sloat argues shockingly that the patterns seen in many evangelical Christian homes are very similar to those seen in the families of alcoholics. He notes four rules of evangelical homes that stifle communication and are clearly dysfunctional.[7]

Rule #1: Don't Say, Do Say

This rule requires that one deny one's true feelings about an issue by not saying what one really thinks or feels. This is systematized dishonesty—an effort to maintain safety or security within the family structure. For Sloat, it is a "subtle rejection of self that pervades the family . . . and is done in such a way that it does not appear damaging because it is presented in the name of God as a spiritual quality." Christian parents (or even cult leaders) can use the biblical admonition of "Children, obey your parents" (Eph. 6:1) as muscle to close a discussion, or to prevent a child from offering his true opinion, or to bring a child into compliance with their wishes.

The "do say" part of the rule further negates one's true opinions and thoughts by compelling one to say what the parent (or leader) wants to hear. In a family it might be making a child say, "Yes, I like that shirt you bought me, Mom," or in a religious cult, "Yes, I am displaying a spirit of discontent." Those who grow up with this rule learn not to value themselves or their own views and beliefs, but instead they attempt to please the authority figures in their lives.

Rule #2: Don't Trust, Do Trust

By trusting others to tell you what to think and believe, but not trusting your *own* opinions or your own ability to think or reason, a psychological "splitting" occurs. This splitting causes one to value the views of others but not to trust one's own internal beliefs and values. In a family this works in many different ways, as when children are discouraged from voicing the doubts they may have about their faith, or their dissatisfaction with the church. If doubt is not worked through within the family, a "splitting" can occur in which a child develops a hypocritical lifestyle. However, when that child is allowed to trust his or her ability to work through seeming contradictions and confused feelings, a true and legitimate faith can emerge. Furthermore, allowing our children to value and trust their own questions and feelings develops in them a more realistic view of their own strengths and weaknesses. This dependency rule can be broken and personal responsibilities can grow into what Donald Sloat calls a "hearty psychological autonomy" when Christian grace, rather than psychological control, is allowed to operate.

Rule #3: Don't Feel, Do Feel

Christian homes like all others can be guilty of discouraging and prohibiting our children from expressing emotions. Another "split" can occur here when an individual has to be "spiritual" in order to live up to the expectations of others. When "control" is the emphasis, such as it is in some families and in most cults, nurture is lost in the process, and children learn to hide their true feelings. The third rule is typified by "don't feel the pain . . . do feel tough and act like I say you should." Some Christian homes and aberrational Christian cultic groups are experts at producing these internal splits, because most individuals want the approval of their parents or their church leaders. For the sake of love and acceptance, they learn to neglect their feelings of anger and betrayal to give the impression that everything is fine. This produces obedient, seemingly healthy followers in a cult group, and "good" children in a family structure. Besides the obvious confusion and hypocrisy that this situation brings, it plays havoc on one's self-concept and the basic need to feel significant and secure.

Rule #4: Don't Want, Do Want

This rule causes an emotional splitting by stating that one shouldn't personally want anything that is against what God wants. Therefore, one must not only give up one's desires, but one should not even *have* desires. Just want what God wants—or what one's parents want, or what one's cultic leader wants. The self is perceived as nearly totally sinful, and so the goal of the good child and true disciple is denial of all personal desires. Sloat states that many in the church community who are "seen as spiritual heroes and selfless givers are actually codependent people who are meeting their own needs by rescuing others." "Spiritual" living under this rule can be destructive in that it keeps people from developing as whole individuals. The "don't want/do want" rule often allows church-going people to deny their legitimate, basic human needs—all in the name of being "spiritual." This causes unnecessary stress, guilt, and self-denial.

True holiness does not oppose personal wholeness. Any type of holiness based on a rigid list of rules that leaves people depressed, unhappy, and wearing a fake smile is neither biblical holiness or psychological wholeness. To be Christ-like is to be both psychologically well-adjusted and holy. It is true that the stress of everyday life, trauma, accidents, illness, and loss can leave anyone sad, depressed, and anxious. That is part of the fallen human condition; through God's grace we can cope with these things. But it is truly worrisome when the depression, sadness, and worry are caused by our efforts to become godly. That is unhealthy both from a spiritual *and* from a psychological sense.

In contrast, healthy homes are characterized by the following, divided into three main categories by Sloat:

I. Basic beliefs (spiritual values)
   The healthy family:
   - provides a shared religious core
   - teaches a sense of right and wrong
   - values service to others
   - admits to problems and seeks help to solve them

II. Interpersonal relationships
   The healthy family:
   - promotes a sense of trust
   - affirms and supports all members
   - fosters communication and listening
   - teaches respect for others
   - respects the privacy of one another

III. General family culture
   The healthy family:
   - balances interaction among members
   - exhibits a sense of shared responsibility
   - displays a sense of play and humor
   - fosters family conversation
   - has a strong sense of family ritual and tradition[8]

In this chapter we have seen that cultists come from all types of families, both healthy and troubled ones. We have also learned that recruitment into a cult is much more likely to happen in association with a severe crisis in a young person's life. Healthy families, as described in the latter portion of this chapter, may be able to do two things to cult-proof their kids that a more dysfunctional family could not. First, a healthier family fosters better communication and is far more likely to know about their child's severe stress and crisis, and they would be talking to that child about it. (Because of the patten of non-communication within the family structure, dysfunctional families may have less chance of even knowing about the crisis.) Second, healthier families are not only more aware of a family member's crisis, but they have also discussed it and provided a sense of comfort and support. Healthier families are also more eager to seek outside professional help to aid their loved one to resolve the personal crisis more completely.

Let me also add that it is quite likely that healthier families have a much greater likelihood of cult-proofing family members from cultic involvement. These families cultivate the tools necessary to educate the family: community, balanced communication, a sense of shared religious morals, and a sense of responsibility to one another. Edith Schaeffer reminds us that a healthy family is "an ecologically balanced environment for the growth of human beings."[9] But the efforts of even the healthiest of families will be thwarted if they are unfamiliar with the dynamics of destructive cults. All of our kids are at risk.

7

PARENTING TIPS

The frightening thing about heredity and environment is that parents provide both.
  —Walter Schreibman in *High Risk:
  Children Without Conscience*

When we are raising our children, there are a number of things we can do to lessen their chances of falling prey to the siren call of cults.

DON'T OVERPROTECT YOUR CHILDREN

A child's personality is determined by a number of factors, the two most important being genetics and parental rearing style. Parents who are overprotective and who teach their children that they can't survive without Mommy or Daddy may inadvertently be creating a situation where the children may become vulnerable to dependency on authority figures. Unscrupulous cult leaders often portray themselves as strong, directive, and nurturing. Your child may never actively seek a *cult*, but if they were overprotected, they may become prey to an authority figure—perhaps a spouse, a boss, or a "friend" who exerts undue control while giving the perception of nurture, love, and acceptance.

ALLOW YOUR CHILDREN TO EXPRESS THEIR THOUGHTS AND EMOTIONS

The Bible clearly teaches children that they are to obey and to be submissive to their parents. However, nowhere does the Bible permit parents to squelch their children's natural curiosity to explore, to think, and to express feelings. Entire nations have become prey to cultic domination because of an extreme emphasis on submission and obedience. In Nazi Germany, obedience to Hitler became the equivalent of obedience to a spiritual leader. Far too often today questioning is viewed as rebelliousness, as it was under Hitler. But it is not necessarily so. The apostle Paul chided the Colossian church for not questioning the unscrupulous leaders who subtly took over the church (Col. 2:8; 16; 18; 20–21). And Paul was exasperated with the Galatians for being "mindless"—the literal meaning of the word translated "foolish" (Gal. 3:1).

Some Christian families feel that certain emotions are absolutely wrong. They may always view anger as a sin, for example. But is it always a sin to be angry? Of course not. Paul indicated that a believer can be angry without sinning (Eph. 4:26). A child scolded for being angry at what she perceives as a response to injustice will feel guilty and confused. If this continues, the angry child will begin to feel like an outcast. She may never develop a healthy self-esteem and instead may compensate by exhibiting various behavior problems.

DON'T OVERCONTROL YOUR CHILDREN

The issue of "control" is a major one for those who have experience in cultic bondage. Why did they let someone "control" them? Often, it's because control occurred in the home long before a child succumbed to cultic control.

When a mother keeps her toddler from running into a busy street, we call that good control, or good parenting. It is part of "training up a child." This is necessary control, motivated by the child's need for protection and safety. But when parents continue to control a child ten, fifteen, or twenty years later, making their daily decisions for them, this is *over* control and usually very manipulative control. If a child continues to develop under such tight oversight, he or she can become an anxious and fearful person, afraid to risk failure, often feeling inadequate and unsure of making their own decisions.

When the child *does* try to act independently, the identity of the parent is undermined, leading to feelings of rejection or betrayal. Even this type of parent's offer of help is often really a disguised attempt to dominate. The parent may feel, "I know what's best for you. I am doing this out of love for you." There is no neutral territory for children with directly controlling parents. If the adult child tries to gain some control over his own life, he pays the price through guilt, often rage, and sometimes deep feelings of disloyalty. There are two common reactions to control: "giving in" and "breaking away."

Sometimes a child raised in a home with at least one dominant overcontrolling parent will "break away" and join a new "family" with "new parents"—sometimes that family may be a cult group. Another controlling parent figure will repeat the internally safe dynamics under which that child was raised.

If you are an overcontrolling, toxic parent[1], you may be setting the stage for your child to become a controller in his or her adult life. Or, your child may become a robotic follower of a cultic leader who provides the same family dynamics that you yourself provided in your child's formative years.

DON'T OVEREMPHASIZE THE VALUE OF OBEDIENCE

Any Christian family will quickly say that "obedience" is one of their primary goals in training their young children. Many believe that if their children learn to obey their parents, promptly and without question, it will ultimately lead to obedience of God. In fact, the leader of the aberrational Christian group that my wife and I were involved in taught that very thing—often and with great vigor. This leader never allowed his children to delay for one moment in following through on a command. Though I certainly do not advocate permissive parenting, nor do I deny the need to respect proper authorities, I cannot state too strongly that obedience only for the sake of obedience inevitably leads to some serious problems in children.

Christian children under overly-strict obedience requirements may not be able to integrate the Christian principles of *why* an act should or should not be done. Furthermore, they may learn to "role play" a proper response without letting their feelings come up to the level of the act, thereby creating the roots of hypocrisy or "emotional splitting" (see chapter five). These children unfortunately may learn "submissiveness" so well that they will not even consider questioning "God's prophet," or some perceived man or woman of God who demands their obedience to whatever is requested as a sign of true submission, loyalty, and godly commitment. Lastly, these children may not develop a healthy conscience of right and wrong if discipline is exercised without consistent boundaries.

Christian families who overemphasize obedience do so at the expense of grace and redemption within the family unit. The lack of freedom and openness may lead to an oppressively rigid system of meeting "godly" goals. Encouraging our children to grow into well-balanced individuals who are obedient to God's call is of course praiseworthy— but the results of trying to achieve this through mindless obedience can be costly.

A number of young women who have come to our retreat center in the past several years were raised in strongly-churched homes, joined nationally known evangelical ministries as young adults, and later joined what they thought were dynamic, growing churches led by vibrant, charismatic leadership-type pastors. Even after several years of their pastors' more solid biblical teachings, they were fairly easily seduced into believing that since God worked so mightily through this pastor, his suggestion for them to have sex with him (to "aid in their spiritual growth") must be obeyed. I do not suggest that obedience was the only factor, but it is nearly impossible to resist anything if "obedience" is linked to your spiritual status.

The fallacious reasoning that "wise men can't be wrong" can lead to the kind of blind obedience that made 913 individuals drink a cyanide-laced fruit drink. Many of the people involved in such groups as the People's Temple in Jonestown, the Jeffrey Lundgren cult murders, the Unification Church, and aberrational Christian groups, will affirm: "We would have done *anything* we were asked to do."

As parents, we should teach obedience, but we should also teach discernment—that is, whom to obey, in which situations, in what ways. Philip Captain, in his book *Eight Stages of Christian Growth*, notes the balanced purpose of obedience: "The goal of the obedience stage is that through the wise use of [the father's] authority the child will come to trust and respect the father leading to willing obedience. The goal of the father is not coerced obedience stemming from the child's fear of the father, but freely chosen obedience stemming from the child's love for the father."[2]

RESPECT YOUR CHILDREN'S DIFFERENT LEARNING STYLES

Some children are more creative, artistic, and intuitive; others are more rigid, analytical, and systematic. Parents should keep two things in mind: Allow and encourage your children to think and express their own opinions. If they are wrong, reinforce the efforts made to reach the conclusion, but then explain why their conclusion was wrong. Then, realize that each child will learn and solve problems differently. It behooves parents to provide the resources, the environment, and the support needed to develop each child's individual learning style properly. In contrast, the cults typically reinforce a single learning style: every cult member will be put into a mold. Diversity is condemned. To cult-proof our kids, we need to teach them that diversity is good. There is diversity in God's creation, the diversity of spiritual gifts, the uniqueness of different members of the body of Christ, and the legitimacy of different points of view on nearly every subject. Farmers are wise enough to handle various seeds differently, so that proper growth and harvest are assured.

ENCOURAGE YOUR CHURCH TO TEACH ABOUT CULTS AND FRINGE CHURCHES

The church can support the training done at home by teaching about cults and apologetics (the defense of Christianity) from the pulpit and through the Sunday school curriculum. A good Sunday school course on cults is *Building Your Christian Defense System*, by Alan and Beth Niquette.[3] While this course lacks any discussion or even acknowledgment of the reality of deceptive mind control, it is one of the few such things available.

DISCIPLINE YOUR CHILDREN, BUT DO NOT ABUSE THEM

There is no clinical evidence or published research to answer the question of how early abuse affects a child's vulnerability to later cultic involvement, but there may be a connection. If you are fearful of abusing your child, either psychologically or physically, seek professional help immediately, both for your child and yourself. If you don't seek help, you may risk very serious and long-lasting legal and psychological problems.

Most parents experience some frustration with disciplining their children. If that is the case for you, seek out support from your church and friends. Find and read books on parenting and discipline. If you find yourself continually irritated and angry with your children, you could need some rest. Parenting is an exhausting business. Do some things *for yourself*—take a break from the twenty-four hour per day devotion to your children.

And don't forget that emotional abuse can be as damaging as physical abuse. Children undergo emotional abuse when they

- are continually yelled at
- are compared with others in an unfavorable light
- are constantly corrected with Bible verses
- are constantly criticized or ridiculed
- receive few, if any compliments
- are lied to by their parents
- are blamed for things that were not their fault
- are given the silent treatment when the parent is angry
- are told not to feel anger—to repress their feelings
- have their salvation questioned.[4]

RECOGNIZE YOUR OWN ADDICTIONS

One can be addicted to more than alcohol or drugs. People can have a compulsive need to work, to have sex, to gamble, or to have relationships with other people. Many Christians are "addicted" to personality cults, following persons of renown or notoriety. If as a parent you are not addicted to any of these things but grew up with addictive parents, you probably have learned some behavioral patterns developed in order to be able to function in the addictive system. You may still be carrying out the same behavioral patterns, even though they may no longer make sense. This problem is especially important when it comes to cults. Cults themselves function very much like an addictive system. If you have been raised in such a system, you or your child may possibly be drawn to a cult out of some vague similarity that cannot be quickly explained— as though something that was missing in your life has now been found.

To recognize the signs of an addictive system is to take steps to correct it. Typical symptoms of addictive families, systems or individuals are as follows:[5]

- lack of real identification with thoughts, emotions, and internal dynamics
- acting from sensory distortion or denial
- sensory input is distorted when received and processed incorrectly
- relationships are dysfunctional; they are based on manipulation
- addictive people or systems have little experience of intimacy
- dependent, they want others to help them
- not liking how they look, they are ashamed to hear what people say to them; they are typically shamed by what they do and who they are

- filled with guilt and feel helpless or powerless
- go from crisis to crisis
- inordinate focus on self
- lack of honesty

GIVE YOUR CHILDREN LOVING AND CORRECT MORAL TRAINING

Children learn morality by what parents do, and not so much by what they say. Interestingly, children tend to be more moral as adults if their parents were warm and loving, regardless of the moral principles directly taught. Parents who are cold and aloof, yet teach much more directly about morality, tend to have less moral children. Still, young people of all persuasions seem to be terribly lacking when it comes to moral reasoning, or knowing why something is good or bad. Today, most people base morality on the influence of the mass media, on popular idols, on peer pressure, or their strong subjective feelings. We need to teach kids *why* moral principles, especially as expounded in the Bible, are correct and practical.

WATCH HOW YOUR CHILD RESPONDS TO DISCIPLINE

James Dobson speaks of the strong-willed child[6]; Ken Magid speaks of a type of child that is even worse, the "trust bandit."[7] These "trust bandits" often become cult leaders or con artists as adults. As children, they are very difficult to discipline. They defy you, stiffen up, and go into rages if their way is thwarted. With the "trust bandit," society may have another con artist or cult leader to worry about.

On the other hand, there are children who may be a bit *too* compliant, a bit *too* good, or a bit *too* sensitive. They desperately cannot stand the feeling of rejection and disapproval. Do they blend into a crowd? Do they avoid initiative? Are they always trying to help others? Are they always being the "pleaser"? If so, they may have a problem as well. They need a bigger dose of self-esteem, and a developed sense of assertiveness. If they don't develop this, they may become prey to the "trust bandits" of the future. In fact, they may have already fallen prey to their stronger, more manipulative peers in their own neighborhoods, classrooms, and churches. The stage is set for deeper exploitation later: the nice daughter may be vulnerable to a male "trust bandit" who makes her believe "He really cared for me, loved me, and treated me like a queen." The nice son may become involved in a cult because the leader "made me feel special; he convinced me I was on a mission for God—that we would do something revolutionary in this generation for the Kingdom of God."

While there is no guarantee that your child will not fall prey to a cult or fringe church, following the ideas outlined above will strengthen their emotional, physical, psychological, moral, and spiritual well-being and most likely will make them less susceptible to the lure of cults.

8

CULT-PROOFING
YOUR SCHOOLS

*Even doctors, in their heyday as god-like paragons,
have never wielded the authority of a single classroom teacher, who can purvey prizes, failure, love,
humiliation and information to great numbers of
relatively powerless, vulnerable young people.*
Marilyn Ferguson, *The Aquarian Conspiracy*

Recently I spoke to a staff person who works with
Campus Crusade for Christ at a university in Ohio. I asked
her if she had seen any changes in students since she began
work on the campus some eight or nine years ago. Without
hesitation she said, "Oh yes, the kids today are more New
Age. They don't believe in the New Age per se, but their
thinking has been deeply influenced by the New Age
philosophy."

The New Age movement draws its beliefs and practices from eastern mysticism and the occult, with an
emphasis on psychic phenomena, astrology, and spiritism.
New Age promoters such as actress Shirley MacLaine and
popular author Matthew Fox teach the essential oneness

and divinity of all creation. They describe the ultimate goal of life as the individual human's realization of his or her own godhood, if not in *this* life, then in a future reincarnation. They emphasize the need for spiritual guidance in this mystical journey by means of submitting to a "spiritual master" or guru, receiving divine wisdom from supernatural beings, "entities," or extra-terrestrials, or through meditative practices.

Subtle New Age thinking is being taught in our local school systems. It is true that there is some controversy in the church about whether these teaching methods can be positive, are wholly negative, or whether they are merely neutral. Yet, if one grants that the methods in themselves are neutral, the problem is still that these things are usually pushed and promoted by those who advocate a New Age worldview. As a consequence, many who practice Eastern methods to achieve altered states of consciousness later come to adopt an Eastern philosophy that is antithetical to Christianity. To cult-proof our children, then, we need to be aware of and combat the New Age thinking in our secular school curriculum.

QUEST

Quest is a joint program of The Quest National Center and the Lions Clubs International. It is packaged as "The Surprising Years," "Skills for Adolescence," or "Skills for Living." A number of organizations that cooperate in Quest are The Center for Early Adolescence, the National Federation for Drug Free Youth, National FTA, the National Middle School Association, and the Pacific Institute for Research and Evaluation.

Increasingly, Quest has come under fire from a number of prominent Christians, including James C. Dobson, who actually had contributed a chapter to an early Quest book. Dobson formally asked to be disassociated from the Quest Program when it became clear to him that Quest was espousing New Age ideas.[1]

The concern over Quest involves a number of issues:

1. Its wholesale borrowing from concepts in the book *Values Clarification* and its strong humanistic emphasis.[2]
2. Its strong implication of the relativism of values, which implies that there are many valid ways to live a good life.[3]
3. The discussion and exercises used in Quest dealing with the concept of death, and the resulting limited and potentially dangerous viewpoints that Quest materials convey about the experience of death.[4]
4. The inappropriate use of personality testing in the "Skills for Adolescence" portion.[5]
5. The lack of parental consent in the "Skills for Adolescent" portion.[6]

For a fuller critique of Quest by Barbara Hanna and Janet Hoover, you may write:

> Pro Family Forum
> P.O. Box 8907
> Ft. Worth, TX 76124

An ongoing battle continues among Quest, various school groups, and individual concerned citizens. Some effort has been made to remove the more objectional components from the curriculum, but this has left many unsatisfied.[7]

GLOBAL EDUCATION

Another insidious infiltration in the public schools comes in the form of Global Education curricula. Generally, Global Education deals with themes involving cultural sensitivity and interdependent cultures, societies, and economics.

One author describes Global Education as "an effort to equip all citizens with the variety of skills and the range of knowledge needed to cope with worldwide economy, scientific potential, and intercultural realities and opportunities."[8]

Global Education is variously named:

- International Studies
- Cultural Awareness
- Futurism
- Multi-cultural International Education
- Global R.E.A.C.H. (Respecting Our Ethnic and Cultural Heritage)
- Project 2000
- Welcome to Planet Earth
- World Core Curriculum[9]

Global Education arose out of a clear need. We now live in a truly international community. World trade has forced us to learn about different cultures, languages, public policies, and values. Increased contact with other nations means we must learn about the cooperation with the people and the institutions of different nations. Eric Buehrer (executive vice-president of Citizens for Excellence in Education), however, points out some of the very real dangers of Globalism, beginning with the fact that Global Education typically paints a bleak, pessimistic view of the world's future, and offers only one solution—a narrow-minded political, psychological, and spiritual alternative.[10] Christians should approach Global Education with extreme caution.

Global Education grossly distorts the values and role of Western Christian civilization, deriding Western values as biased, bigoted, and the chief source of the world's contemporary problems.

Globalists teach relativism, that is, that there are no absolute values. To world problems globalism advocates politically liberal, extremist solutions. Some Globalists even see a future being capably managed by those advocating and practicing a brand of Eastern mysticism.

Globalists tend to use such Eastern concepts as *karma*—that one's acts, thoughts, and attitudes have their consequences in this life and the life to come; and *reincarnation*—that after death all humans are reborn in subsequent rounds of births and deaths, depending on how righteous one was in one's previous life. Other Eastern-mystical concepts frequently taught as part of the globalist curriculum are the concept of *prana*. Prana is the idea that everything is a form of energy, and that this energy form is a "god." Globalists may also introduce the concept of *maya*, though perhaps without actually using the term. Maya means "illusion," and it refers to the Hindu teaching that the world is illusory. We mortals merely see the world out of spiritual delusion. The true essence of the world is Brahman, or absolute reality. We must be liberated from all illusion and ignorance, so that we can see the reality or Brahman.

Western Judeo-Christian values are being systematically stripped from our textbooks. Relativism is the secular worldview of choice, and it is being taught almost exclusively in many school curricula. Solutions to global problems are virtually always seen from a leftist viewpoint. World problems are attributed to capitalism, imperialism, and nationalism. Little is said of the dangers of communism or totalitarianism.[11]

Robert Mueller, United Nations Undersecretary for the Economic and Social Council, has written a Global Education book entitled *New Genesis: Shaping a Global*

Spirituality. There is no pretext here. His New Age approach to spirituality is obvious—and this spirituality is clearly Eastern. For Mueller the solution lies in the Hindu teachings of *karma* and *prana.*[12]

Mueller's book is now part of the curriculum of the School of Ageless Wisdom, which is also being called The Robert Mueller School. This school, based in Texas, has emphasized traditional occultic teachings in its curriculum, the specific occultic base of the school being found in the teachings of Alice A. Bailey, a spiritualistic channeler of the early twentieth century. Bailey transformed messages from Eastern gurus and masters into "nectar" suited to thirsty minds in the West. She claimed that the earth is ruled by a spirit, a Sanat Kumara, Lord of the World, who came to the earth millions of years ago. The Mueller School curriculum distills this hidden knowledge so that the ignorant minds of the West can once again be enlightened. The Southern Association of Colleges and Schools (SACS) is highly impressed with Mueller's program—New Age thinking and all. The SACS reported that "The most current education processes recommended by the most advanced research on mind, brain and human development are being used to enhance the mental, physical, and spiritual development of each child." And the association is also on record as having said that "The Robert Mueller School is an exceptional model in our contemporary world. We the committee have recommended that information about the school's educational processes be shared with educators as much as possible."[13]

OTHER NEW AGE INFLUENCES

Other overt forms of New Age influence can also be seen in public schools. These include forms of Eastern meditation, yoga, and occultic practices. Some eastern meditation practices teach children to contact their "spirit guides." Generally these meditative practices encourage a combination of muscle relaxation, exercise, controlled breathing, and a focusing of the mind either on nothingness, or on something within the one meditating—whether it be the spirit guide, the inner self, the god within, a mysterious word or sound, or perhaps something else, like a baffling riddle. Yoga is actually a part of meditation exercise. "Yoga," a Hindu term meaning to "yoke," refers to a harnessing of one's personal powers by way of breathing, exercise, and posture. In traditional Hinduism, the yoga process was always for the purpose of becoming "enlightened," or coming into oneness ("union") with god.

Occultic practices can involve astrology, divination, magic, witchcraft, or contact with the dead. "Occult" means "secret" or "hidden," and the purpose of occultism is to gain control or power over one's self or over others through hidden knowledge. Some advocates of the New Age program deliberately try to disguise the occultic nature of their supposedly innocuous educational philosophy so as to gradually convince the "old guard" of social and educational officials that the program is inoffensive. They feel obligated to compromise and "tone down" their direct approach by using indirect techniques. To promote their agenda, they will often avoid references to metaphysical principles unfamiliar to the Western, European tradition.[14]

WHAT YOU CAN DO

Many are concerned about such New Age influence in the schools. Former Secretary of Education William Bennett is one of them:

> Another legacy from the Age of Aquarius that has been enshrined in too many of our social studies curricula is a disturbing antirational bias. Curriculum

guides for . . . global education are shot through with calls for "raised consciousness," for students and teachers to view themselves "as passengers on a small cosmic spaceship," for classroom activities involving "intuiting," "imaging," or "visioning" a "preferred future."

Two proponents of such curricula have offered a candid caution: "These exercises may seem dangerous to your logical thought patterns. For best results, suspend your judging skills and prepare to accept ideas that seem silly and/or impractical." Well, if we're going to give up critical judgment, we'd better give up the game of education altogether.[15]

A report prepared by Greg Cunningham for the United States Department of Education outlines some of the dangers of Global Education programs and their lack of balance.[16] While a shorter version of the report can be found in other sources,[17] the complete document can be purchased through Citizens for Excellence in Education (see address below).

Given the subtle, yet nevertheless pervasive and potentially harmful New Age influence in the schools, how can parents cult-proof their kids against New Age thinking or other forms of cultic influence?

- Be informed about what is taught in your child's public school curriculum.
- Review the books, articles, flyers, or movies that your child receives or watches, and explain how this material is often one-sided—and sometimes shows no respect for the teachings of Christianity.
- Familiarize yourself and your child with alternative material concerning Global Education and the New Age Movement.
- Be informed of the work done by groups such as:

The National Association of Christian Educators—
Citizens for Excellence in Education (NACE-CEE)
P.O. Box 3200
Costa Mesa, California 92628 (714) 546-5931

- Review the source material in *A Parent's Handbook
  for Identifying New Age Religious Beliefs, Psycho-
  therapeutic Techniques, and Occult Practices in
  Public School Curriculums.* To obtain this book,
  write to:
  The Ankerberg Theological Research Institute
  P.O. Box 8977
  Chattanooga, TN 37411 (615) 892-7722

- Write your local PTA, school board, or congressional representative regarding the infiltration of Global Education, New Age, and occult-influenced
  curriculum in your schools.

- Stay abreast of books and articles covering the New
  Age influence in the schools.[18]

- Develop critical thinking skills in yourself and your
  child. Schools often do little to teach children
  critical thinking skills. For more on developing
  critical thinking, see chapter 9.

9

DEVELOPING CRITICAL THINKING SKILLS

What luck for the rulers that men do not think.
—Adolf Hitler

Allan Bloom, professor of humanities at the University of Chicago and author of *The Closing of the American Mind*, wrote his book as "a meditation on the state of our souls, particularly those of the young and their education."[1] He says that in our modern colleges and universities, "almost every student entering the university believes, or says he believes, that truth is relative."[2]

What are some of the conclusions of the relativism as taught in our schools? A student trained in relativism is taught that all the wars in the past were fought over the foolish notion that there was some truth, some standard worthy of defense. In fact, all society's ills—"wars, persecution, slavery, xenophobia, racism, and chauvinism"—are laid on the altar of absolutistic thinking.[3]

Because of relativistic thinking, the Judeo-Christian ethic is slowly being replaced by a new social ethic. Now, instead of The Ten Commandments, we have values clarification (or, as Ted Koppel once said on "Nightline," *The Ten Suggestions*); instead of abortion being a wrongful taking of innocent human life, we have "a woman's right to choose"; instead of calling homosexuality a sin or even a psychological disorder, it is now described as an alternate lifestyle or "sexual preference"; and instead of hailing people who refuse to rent an apartment to unwed couples as heroes of traditional values, society calls them bigots, narrow minded, and intolerant.

The examples are legion, but my point is that all of these things are products of an educational system that has thrown the concept of truth and absolutes out the door.

CRITICAL THINKING SKILLS

Cult researchers Bob and Gretchen Passantino note that the lack of teaching in the critical thinking area makes two kinds of Christians: those who do not think at all and consequently do not worship and serve God with their minds; and those who attempt to use their minds but end up making mistakes that could be avoided by learning how to think straight.[4]

In order to cult-proof our kids, and in order to combat the relativisitic thinking they will encounter at school, we need to teach them basic critical thinking skills. Following are some basic concepts that will help you and your child think clearly and critically about complex issues.

The Law of Non-Contradiction

The law of non-contradiction states that two contrary propositions cannot be true, but they both can be false.

While a doctoral student at the University of Pittsburgh, I was discussing my belief in Christianity with some others. A fellow student argued, "That's a truth for *you*. For *you* it is true, but it is not *my* truth." This student abandoned the law of non-contradiction. Christianity cannot be true and other religions true also. Christianity cannot be true for me if it is not true for everyone; it cannot be true if other religions are also true. All religions can be false, but all religions cannot be true. One cannot hold that Jesus Christ is the single path to God on the one hand, and on the other hand believe that there are many ways to God.

"Christian" cults typically ignore the law of non-contradiction. That is, they ignore contradictions. For example, when group members criticize others, they are "judging," but when a *leader* criticizes someone, he or she is "discerning." Cult members do not encourage you to weigh one teaching against another, nor do they even care if someone is brought to Christian faith; all they care about is whether others are joining their *group*. In their mind, anyone outside the group, even Christians, are "lost." The mind of cultists is held in constant confusion, and for them to recover, the contradictions must be exposed and the cultist must recognize the inconsistencies.

Moral Truths Are Not Matters of Taste

The Christian moral code is not unique. A similar code is found in every major religion of the world. All believe that lying, cheating, stealing, murder, adultery, are wrong. Similarly, variations of the "Golden Rule" are found in the Jewish Talmud, the Hindu *Mahabharata*, the Buddhist Sutras, and the sacred texts of Confucianism, Jainism, and Taoism.[5]

Cults nearly always set up *new* moral standards. Issues of taste and preference and conscience, things such as use of makeup, clothing styles, dating, the amount of time devoted to religious activities, and the number of children to have, are all relegated to a new "moral code." Christians need to be taught what is and what is not part of the essential moral code. Is dancing a sin, or is fudging a bit on one's income tax returns? Focusing on tastes or preferences only sets people up to follow the newest craze in moral do's and don'ts. These sorts of moral codes constantly change and become trendy.

Similar Does Not Prove Same

Because something is *like* something else, that does not mean that it is identical to that other thing; pandas *look* like bears and are often called panda bears, but they are actually related to raccoons.

In their book *Witch Hunt*, the Passantinos point out that some people in anti-cult movements use sloppy reasoning by unfairly castigating cults, or lumping legitimate groups together with cults.[6] They are correct. "Similar does not prove same" corrects that error. If something is similar to something else, that does not mean that it must be identical or that it came from the same source. Take for example those groups that practice "shepherding." I have heard the erroneous conclusion that all shepherding groups are the same—and even that they were all influenced by the "Fort Lauderdale Five"[7] or by Juan Carlos Ortiz, people active in the shepherding movement. But in fact, some groups developed "shepherding" concepts and techniques quite independently of one another, and the actual practices of shepherding groups *do* differ significantly in what and how shepherding concepts are taught. That is not to say, however, that there are not dangers in the so-called "shepherding movement." But one must be careful to identify a group's methods, their history, and the resulting potential harm.

Cults and cultic organizations will point to certain other groups, churches, pastors, or denominations and say, "They're not doing evangelism the same way we are, so they're not doing anything to preach the gospel." If the listener hears this enough, he or she will erroneously conclude that *no* church is doing anything regarding evangelism except their own. Naturally, evidence to the contrary is never cited by cult leaders, and members are never encouraged to go searching for it.

Either/Or Thinking

It is erroneous to believe people have only two options.[8] There are *always* other options. One leader of a fringe church kept a member in the group by reminding him how horrible his family was, convincing the person that the only option he had if he left the group was to return to his family. Once the young man finally realized he was in a cult and wanted to leave, he was faced with the terrifying prospect of returning to his dysfunctional family. During counseling he began to see that there were other options. Did he *have* to move home? Couldn't his parents change? Did he have to accept the negative images of himself he received as a child? Once these options were seen, the sense of being trapped vanished.

Cults often teach that you are either with them or against them, and that if you are against them, God will destroy you, or you will be attacked by demons. To refute this reasoning, former members must see that their eternal destiny does not depend on loyalty to a group, or what a particular group teaches about salvation. Instead, they always have other choices.

Either/or thinking is also practiced by aberrational groups in their views of criticism and praise. Any criticism from outsiders is always considered persecution. Praise is considered a sign of God's favor. This thinking warps the mind, keeps cultists unable to question critically, and eliminates viable options.

False Analogy

A "false analogy" occurs when people incorrectly reason that if things are alike or similar in several areas, then they must be alike or similar in all areas.[9]

Cults use false analogy in a number of innovative and destructive ways. For example, a critic of a cultic Pentecostal sect, the House of Agape of Lawrence, Kansas, was judged untrustworthy because he had a blemish on his arm. How did the Pentecostal cult leader come to this decision? All physical imperfections are a sign of disease. Disease is under the domain of sin and Satan. Satan causes disease. A blemish is an imperfection, and thus a type of disease. Therefore, this critic must be of Satan. Therefore, "we don't have to listen to him." Even if one grants the preposterous assumption that blemishes are of the devil, it still does not follow in any logical way whatsoever that the criticism itself was wrong! Such false analogy also usually involves the old error *argumentum ad hominem*: discrediting a person's argument by discrediting the person.

During the time I was a member of the Great Commission International, leaders were asked to "step down" from leadership because some of their disciples were doing poorly. The leadership reasoned that poor fruit is a sign of a poor tree. Therefore, if there are any weak disciples, then there must be a poor tree. This leader must go. And Scripture was used to justify the false analogy, for they would quote, "A tree is known by its fruit." But wait a minute. Look at some leaders in the Bible. Some of the disciples stopped following Jesus (see John 6). Peter denied Christ, and Judas betrayed him. Paul saw entire churches desert him. Moses endured several full-scale rebellions against his authority, thousands of his followers turning aside to worship idols.

Cults ruin reputations by using false analogy. They

will point to a fault here or a fault there in a person, and then conclude erroneously that the person is bad. I have actually heard good, solid ministries discredited by comments like, "Oh, I wouldn't listen to him. He didn't even give a clear altar call tonight. This man doesn't preach the gospel." By false analogy one concludes an entire ministry is compromised and unspiritual.

The Appeal to Authority

How many times have we all heard, "Well, our *pastor* says," or "our *elders* believe," or "Reverend So-and-So doesn't believe that way." This tactic is used all the time in advertising. An actor talks about how good his Toyota, or Chrysler, or whatever, is. But wait. Is this actor an expert on cars? Is he an engineer, or a professional car driver? No. One's celebrity has no logical connection to the value of the car. It would be just as valuable or maybe more valuable if my *neighbor* recommended a car.

Cultists are quite vulnerable to this error. They are taught to believe without questioning. What makes their pastor an authority? What gives an untrained and unaccredited pastor the right to disagree with two thousand years of church tradition, throwing out the Apostles' Creed or anything else that he does not like or agree with? Simply because someone is a pastor does not make him or her an expert on matters of the church, nor does that title automatically confer proper training or educational qualifications. The pastor then has no authority about what car to buy, where to live, what type of tea to purchase, or what type of grass seed is best for your lawn. The pastor is not an expert in these areas.

I have worked with hundreds of former members, and I can see this appeal to authority being made by virtually every cult leader. All appeal to their *own* authority. They will tell you they are God's servants. Why? They say, "Because I tell you I am—God told me." *Anyone* could make the same claim. What makes their claim truthful? Hundreds of cult leaders claim to be God's anointed prophet in the end times, each one doing things differently from the rest of the leaders *also* claiming to be God's anointed for these last times. One says, "God told me we can't evangelize any more because the 'door of grace has been closed.'" Another says, "God has anointed me to take the gospel to the ends of the earth in these last days." Still another says, "God has shown me the vision, the secret strategy to reach the world for Christ in this generation."

Many in the cults appeal to their leaders. "Brother Smith says," or "Bishop Thistlethwaite proclaimed," or "Pastor Congoleum declared." What matters is not what somebody said but whether what they say squares with the Word of God and with the historic creeds of the church. Ask questions! *Truth is truth.* It is not fragile; it can stand examination, verification, even vilification. Truth stands tall and proud in the free marketplace of ideas.

RECOMMENDED READING

If you would like to sharpen your critical thinking skills, you may want to read the following books:

- *The Abolition of Man*, by C. S. Lewis (New York: Macmillan, 1947). This classic exposes the illogical, faulty principles of modern education. Lewis wrote this book in the 1940s, and few have really taken note of his prophetic warnings.
- *The Closing of the American Mind*, by Allan Bloom (New York: Simon & Schuster, 1987). Bloom, professor of Humanities at the University of Chicago, exposes the errors of relativism.
- *Truth in Religion*, by Mortimer J. Adler (New York:

Macmillan, 1990). Adler rescues religious truth from the viewpoint that one should pick religious preferences like one expresses a preference in desserts. Adler does not clearly state which religion is true, but he does rule out Eastern religions because at their core they embrace absolutely contradictory claims about reality.

- *The Manipulators*, by Everett L. Shostrom and Dan Montgomery (Nashville: Abingdon Press, 1990). This book is an excellent introduction to helping people recognize the signs of manipulation by others. The book points out that manipulation is a tool to keep people from being who they really are. In essence, manipulation is a type of lie.
- "The Poison of Subjectivism," by C. S. Lewis, is a brief essay that appears in *Christian Reflections* (Grand Rapids: Eerdmans, 1967). He points out the bankruptcy of thinking with no absolutes, arguing that those who try to overthrow traditional morality have no basis remaining even to judge the rightness or wrongness of traditional morality, let alone to suggest its replacement.

10

CULTS AND FRIENDSHIPS

More than any other factor, the desire for uncompli-
cated warmth and acceptance seems to lead people
into cults. Indeed, there is much evidence to suggest
that the cults understand this need and work hard to
fulfill it.

—Rachel Andres and James Lane,
Cults and Consequences

In my sophomore year at a large university, I became
the "freak" of the dorm—all because I was an admitted
Christian. I never walked down the halls with my Bible. I
never preached on the street corners, or even evangelized
my fellow students. Yet my Christianity was discussed and
ridiculed in dorm bull sessions.

Several times my dorm room was filled to overflowing
with students who wanted to see me debate the "dorm
theologian," a guy who had once attended a seminary
somewhere. While in seminary this student had been
"enlightened" concerning the true nature of the Bible and
theology. Summoned forth to correct my "primitive"

thinking, he lectured me on the Bible being a bunch of myths and stories. Of course, all the other students took his side, laughing when I tried to defend my faith.

My experience with the professors was no better. Many professors used their classes as pulpits to vilify God, Jesus Christ, miracles, and especially Christians. During a philosophy class, a Jewish student and I tried to make a case for God's existence. We both became objects of ridicule, and I began to feel alone and unsupported as a Christian.

My experience with churches during this crucial time was not much better. While I was not a target of ridicule at the church, even there I had no sense of connectedness or belonging to any Christian community. As a single person, I often walked over from my dormitory to attend a nearby church of one of the historic denominations. In the two years I regularly attended there, I desperately wished some family would invite me over for a Sunday meal. In two years, no one from those churches invited me to anything. The pastor never called on me.

After I married, my wife and I faithfully attended a Bible church for two years. One time after church an older couple told us, "It's so nice to see you young folks here. We hope you come back." We had attended regularly for *two years*. It seemed that no one even noticed us! Neither did the pastor of that church ever call on us. No one ever even tried to get to know us.

Then along came Great Commission International. My wife and I joined, for it seemed to offer something that the church didn't: friendship. Here were people my age, from similar backgrounds, and they were very committed Christians. They sang popular folk songs, drove around in a VW van, and they witnessed for Christ. They lived a simple life which they were willing to share. Most important, they seemed to care for me.

Like me, most people join fringe groups to overcome a

sense of isolation and loneliness. In fact, eminent scholar Hannah Arendt, in her famous book *The Origins of Totalitarianism*, argues that the "preconditions for total domination" are isolation and loneliness.[1] The preconditions for political totalitarianism as well as for religious cultism are really quite similar. The dynamics of power and control in one is reflected in the other. In fact, the pioneering work on religious cultism was done by scholars studying brainwashing and totalitarianism in the early 1950s. To their amazement, they saw a type of brainwashing exhibited in cult members that was nearly identical to the brainwashing seen in those subjected to thought reform programs in totalitarian societies.[2]

Why, then, if most people join cults to escape loneliness and isolation, do these symptoms reappear once they have involved themselves in a cult? It is because these friendships have only the appearance, but none of the reality, of true friendships.

CHARACTERISTICS OF CULTIC FRIENDSHIPS

Cult members seem to be friendly, caring, sensitive, and honest. In reality, however, they are often dishonest, manipulative, and destructive. The following examples show the characteristics of cultic friendships.

Cultic Friendships Do Not Encourage Honesty and Openness

Rules in cult life often produce a self that cannot be open. You are told whom you are to see and when to see them. You are told what to read, what to hear, what to think. You are told what is right and what is wrong. The cultic influence produces a restricted self.

Some areas of the self that cults deny or label "sinful" include:

- Certain pleasure and activities like visiting parents, taking vacations, going to movies, seeing old friends, pursuing a career.
- Certain thoughts and feelings, such as:
  - Something is wrong with this group.
  - I don't want to go to another meeting.
  - I'm tired of the constant prayer, evangelism, Bible study, and group fellowship.
  - I really have special feelings for this person.
  - I don't know if I agree with that teaching or not.
  - I am tired and discouraged.
  - I don't feel like meditating today.
  - What does our group do with all the money we take in?

The consequences of giving up openness, honesty, and the vital aspects of one's true personality are serious. Cultic relationships cannot be totally open and honest. One way to cult-proof your child is to encourage them to find friends who will encourage and welcome honesty and openness.

We ought to teach our kids to be wary of people who say, "You shouldn't feel that way." We can feel any way we want to feel. If you open up to someone and share your feelings, and that person disapproves, the fault is theirs, not yours. We don't need to have the identical worldview to everyone else.

In my private practice I have counseled many Christians who have been deeply wounded by other Christians who told them their depression was a sin. The message that the depressed one hears is, "Good Christians are not depressed," or even more devastating, "Don't be honest with me." The truth is that Christians *do* get depressed—and they get angry, sad, and anxious, just like everyone else. Jesus himself was discouraged about his efforts to call Israel to repentance, and he was angry at the money changers in the temple, yet he was without sin.

In actuality, if you are not open and you are dishonest with your feelings and thoughts, then you are a hypocrite. A plastered-on smile that hides intense inner problems is no testimony to a life changed by Christ's grace. In my clinical work I would much rather see someone be open and honest about depression or anger and show a desire to face up to it rather than deny it. "Facing ourselves does not mean we take total responsibility for a failing relationship [or a conditional friendship in a cultic group]. Rather it means we take total responsibility for ourselves in the relationship."[3]

Few people complain and are negative because they enjoy it. Most are crying out for help, attention, understanding, and appreciation. The Scriptures clearly instruct us to encourage the timid or fainthearted, and to help the weak (1 Thess. 5:14). How can we ever encourage or help anyone if they are too afraid or too ashamed to open up? So we need to encourage our children to ask themselves, "Do my friends encourage openness and honesty and not hold it against me when I offer it?"

CULTIC FRIENDSHIPS ARE ONE-WAY RELATIONSHIPS

Poor friendships are marked by an imbalance. One person is always giving more than the other. Alfred Ells, in his book, *One Way Relationships—When You Love Them More Than They Love You*, notes the symptoms of a "one-way codependency" with a friend. To determine whether you or your child may be involved in this type of relationship, just answer the following questions (the more characteristics you match, the more codependent or unhealthy the relationship is likely to be):

119

- Do you consistently love, care, or take more responsibility than the other person?
- Do you "tiptoe" around the person for fear of what might be said, done, or felt?
- Do you have difficulty being totally honest, direct, and loving in your communication with your friend?
- Do you spend time second-guessing their motives, needs, or actions?
- Do you cover, lie, excuse, or in other ways justify another's behavior to yourself or to someone else?
- Do you find yourself being regularly critical, blaming, or negative toward the person?
- Do you feel the need to convince the person that you are right and they are wrong?
- Do you constantly feel the need to give in—or give up—just to keep the peace?
- Do you have trouble maintaining a steady emotional life when another person goes up or down?
- Do you worry, obsess, or become tormented about that person or your relationship?
- Are you always the one to first admit you're wrong, and then apologize or beg in order to resolve conflicts?
- Are you the one who always has to go "the extra mile" to make the relationship work?"[4]

Often a person in this kind of relationship denies that there is a problem. But, as Alfred Ells says, "Denial soothes our senses but keeps us in bondage. The truth hurts in a one-way relationship, but it will set you free."[5]

Cultic Friendships Do Not Affirm Your Talents and Interests

God gave us all unique talents and interests which should not be suppressed or denied. Theresa, a girl from

New York, wanted to sing and act, but her friends thought singing and acting were stupid, and they made fun of her. She was told to do something more practical instead. She never felt affirmed. True friends would have affirmed Theresa and tried to help her pursue her dreams. Theresa may never become a professional singer or actress, but failing to realize a dream is never an excuse to not develop and cultivate our talents to the best of our abilities and desires. Friends who recognize and encourage this in one another are real friends.

Cultic Friendships Discourage Your Relationships with Friends and Family

As a rule, cults and cult-like organizations do little to encourage relationships with friends and parents. I have counseled a number of families who actually hired private investigators and contacted the police or FBI in order to locate their child. The friends that their son or daughter made while in the cult viewed any family problem as an excuse to completely avoid the family. No family is perfect, but cults will typically exploit even a minor weakness in family relationships in order to convince the family member to make a clean break. These young people are told that their families are "evil" and that they will prevent them from performing the "crucial mission" that God has called them to do. Kids can be cult-proofed by being taught to beware of any "friend" who suggests that their parents are evil.

Sadly, some kids join cults because they have no family. The cult *becomes* their family. Some homes are so dysfunctional and abusive that children leave them in order to survive. In other homes, the courts remove the child. Few young people want to be loners. Most search for friends and a substitute family. These children are often at even higher risk than others, for in their effort to find a substitute family or new set of friends, they will compromise the guidelines and allow others to suppress or silence them.

Cultic Friendships Try to Change Your Personality

Cults typically attack an individual's personality. People differ in their temperaments, interests, talents, and abilities. However, cult groups ignore these differences. Instead, they are focused on a goal or vision to which members must conform. To build up the group, the members must be aggressive recruiters through evangelism and outreach. Very often this goal becomes more important than the needs of the individual. Introverts—those who prefer to be alone and engage in individual activities—are told that this is sin, and that not attending all the meetings and church activities is being selfish. In truth, it may not be selfish at all. It could well be that the person is better using her talents and interests by staying away from some of the group activities and doing something on her own. The reverse happens in cults that emphasize meditation, devotion, and the inner life. They tend to make the *extrovert* feel less spiritual. In both cases, the agenda of the cults is to distort personality.[6]

A normally functioning personality is like a tire that is properaly inflated and so can function smoothly. Too little air in the tires will make them wear out and make steering difficult and dangerous; too much air inflation may cause a rough ride or even a blowout.

In the same way, personalities can be restricted—or, to use our tire analogy, have "too little air." Christie was convinced by the leader of her group that it was God's will that she help with his family's child care, cleaning, and cooking. To be "godly," she had to work without complaint or question. When she had negative thoughts about her job, she was taught to tell herself, "I'm being selfish and not being very Christ-like. I must repent of this attitude and try to rejoice."

Christie endured this year after year. Her dreams of college and a career in music were slipping away. She grew extremely depressed and suicidal. Her cult leader chided her for not rejoicing and for not doing enough around the house. Finally she could take it no longer. She reasoned, "If I am going to hell anyway for my unrepentant attitude, I'll be a lot happier on earth doing something else." So Christie left the abusive group and eventually found her way to Wellspring. She learned that her desires for college and music were not sinful. Christie is now in college and no longer depressed, and she has helped many others overcome their cult experiences.

Christie's story is a typical example of what it is like to live in a personality-constricting cult. Her personality was constricted not because she wasn't a good cook and housekeeper, but because she was not allowed the *full expression* of her personality and talent.

The personality expanders do the opposite of the personality constrictors. Instead of *denying* parts of the personality, like musical appreciation or artistic expression, they *encourage* or even *enforce* members to become something that they are not. In this way—to return to the tire analogy—they put *too much* air into the tire.

In the personality-expanding type of experience, cult leaders get people to do things they really *don't* have the ability or psychological wherewithal to do. For example, one early teaching of Great Commission International was that every brother should become an elder.[7] The leader reasoned that "elder" meant "mature." Since every Christian is to be mature, then every young man is eventually to become an elder. Those lacking in spiritual leadership gifts and desire were consequently viewed as immature—and immaturity for those who had been in Great Commission for a number of years was simply a form of disobedience. Many young men agonized over the fact that they were not becoming "mature." The pressure on some of them was more than they could bear. Some dropped out, bitter and disillusioned about Christianity. Others struggled with their identity and vocational pursuits for ten to fifteen years after leaving the movement—all because the group had pushed them into areas where they didn't have the talent to perform.

Cultic friendships, then, will often either restrict or expand the group member's personality—with damaging psychological results.

Cultic Friendships Try to Change Your Morality

Morality is also altered in the cults. Groups often try to stretch morals by encouraging (or permitting) lying, adultery, fornication, and extortion. Some cultic groups in this country have even required murder.

Christians have a general understanding of what is defined as sin, and whatever is outside the boundaries of sin is considered to be in the realm of human freedom. In the area of human freedom one can do as one chooses, so long as it is not personally harmful or harmful to others.

Cults, however, *expand* the definition of sin—even if they do not use the word *sin*. They may refer to the "lower self," rebellion, negative energies, evil, an independent spirit, or lack of Christ consciousness. And there are some groups that do not acknowledge *any* concept analogous to sin. However, most cults do have certain explicit or implicit lists of do's and don'ts. So these cults in essence define new sins into existence. Here are some sins or evils that my clients were taught in their respective groups:

- Sleeping too much
- Visiting parents
- Using makeup
- Using versions of the Bible other than the King James Version
- Refusing to have sexual relations with the leader
- Not going to the bathroom when told
- Raising less than the expected amount of money each day
- Missing meetings
- Questioning the leader
- Feeling tired
- Showing anger
- Revealing any longing for home or pleasant memories of the past
- Missing parents and other family members

Some cults also *limit* or *narrow* what is considered to be sin. Here, things that have traditionally been viewed as sin, such as murder, adultery, or theft are no longer thought of as sins in every instance. They are now considered a means to use when necessary in order for the group to achieve its goals.

A tragic example of cults changing one's morals is the case of Jeffrey Lundgren, a lay preacher in the Reorganized Church of Jesus Christ of Latter Day Saints who broke from his church in Kirtland, Ohio, proclaiming himself to be God's prophet for these end times. He ordered a family of five to be killed, and one member of the cult, Danny Kraft, Jr., was so brainwashed by Lundgren that to this hour he feels Lundgren is the prophet of God and that he acted properly in assisting in the killing of the Avery family.

I worked with Danny before and during the ensuing trial. At first Danny proclaimed his and Jeffrey's innocence. But the more I listened to Danny the more I realized that he was using words in a most unusual manner. Cults at times often develop their own language, using the standard English vocabulary but with altered meanings. So it was with Danny. He would use words like *judgment, justice,* and *punishment,* then tell his attorney and me that he didn't know what happened to the Averys. Finally I realized he was actually telling us that he could not understand why the family had not listened to the prophet, Jeffrey Lundgren. He was able to proclaim his innocence because in his mind he did not actually murder the Averys. Rather, he executed God's judgment. *God* killed the Averys, claimed Danny.

Danny grew up like most children. He was normal for his age, bright, friendly, and helpful. He had tremendous artistic talent. During the course of preparing for his trial over sixty people from his hometown in Illinois were interviewed. Teachers, friends, neighbors, and relatives were consulted. They all told the same story: Danny was a normal boy. They were absolutely shocked that Danny would be involved in the murder of an entire family.

I saw the tears and the deep grief of his parents as they testified in the courtroom. Danny's dad had gone to the police, to the pastors of the Kirtland church, and to the FBI. He knew something was wrong with his son because Danny didn't write or come home to visit any more. His personality had changed. His sense of humor was gone. But the authorities in Kirtland, Ohio, dismissed Mr. Kraft's concerns. And so Danny Kraft, Jr., was tried and convicted on five counts of kidnapping and five counts of aggravated murder.

This is a graphic example of what can happen in a cult. Danny's story is an illustration of what can happen when the boundaries for right and wrong are violated by cult leaders.

ENCOURAGING HEALTHY FRIENDSHIPS IN YOUR CHILDREN

What has been said about personality and sin and how cults can expand or constrict both of these, depending on their own agenda, should sensitize parents to how cults can exploit our children. I recommend that we all educate our children about boundaries as they relate to sin and to a healthy personality. Reinforce your child. Affirm his identity and individual personality. Talk to your child about right and wrong. Does she know the boundaries? Can your child spot so-called friends who want to violate the boundaries in regard to sin and to personal identity?

As a parent, you want to encourage your children to have healthy friendships and relationships: friends who are honest and open, who share in a mutual give-and-take, who affirm your child's talents and interests, who encourage your child to relate to you and other family members, who enjoy your child's personality, and who strengthen your child's morals.

Not all friends your child makes should be on the same level, however. Encourage friendships on three levels—those who are ahead, equal to, and behind your child spiritually, emotionally, and intellectually. Proper growth requires all three types of friends.[8]

We all need friends who are more advanced spiritually, emotionally, and intellectually than we are because they provide us with good examples. However, an exclusive focus on people who are ahead of us in these areas may make us feel inadequate. Therefore we need other friends at our own level intellectually, spiritually, and emotionally. These peer friends are hard to find, but they are a great encouragement to us because we can be so honest with them. It is hard to be honest with our role models because we are not at their level yet.

Finally, we need friends we can help and serve. With friends "behind" us, our skills, compassion, and Christian charity can really be exercised. We can provide for these friends the listening ear, the love, and the understanding that was sometimes never afforded them by others. Many of us have been on the receiving end of this kind of friendship. But we need to be wary and to set limits. Don't encourage pity parties—constantly allowing people to vent their emotions, cry, and complain. Sometimes it is our responsibility as a friend to gently confront, set limits, or even encourage others to seek professional counseling.

Encourage Your Children to Be Open with You

Be open and honest with your children about the associations they choose. Help them to realize when friends or others begin to stifle their ability to think freely, to feel emotions, and to express themselves. And be sure to develop healthy friendships in your own life. Your model and instruction will provide the best examples for your children as they develop their own relationships.

Know If Your Child Is a Leader or a Follower

Being a leader or a follower is not a sign either of strength or weakness. Some of us essentially are leaders, and others are closer to follower-type personalities. Each personality type has its own vulnerabilities, and it is important to review these vulnerabilities with your child. For example, followers may be too easily prone to give up their own values, feelings, and aspirations in favor of what others want. This can bring undue anxiety, depression, and ambivalence. Some children will never be leaders—and they should not feel guilty about it. If they are followers, they should be given tools to assess *who* to follow and *how much* to follow. Those who have follower-type personalities can serve and help, but it is also their responsibility to avoid being manipulated by leaders.

By the same token, if your child is a budding leader type, he or she should learn not to exploit others. True leaders must be sensitive to other personality styles and talents, and they should remember that in leading others they must serve them and nurture them. Point your child to Christ as the model leader, for better than any other model he shows that the purpose of leadership is service. To serve, we must know well whom we are serving. People must be treated as individuals, according to their personality type. As Stan Mooneyham writes:

> The destined goal [of the leader] is not to reduce everyone to a common denominator personality but to elevate everyone to a fully alive, fully contributing personality. The need is not to subdue personality but to Christianize it. Jesus didn't try to make carbon copies out of the men he chose. The leader who diminishes his followers does not pass the test.[9]

Assess Whether Your Child Has a Dependent Personality

If a person is consistently dependent and submissive, they are very likely a dependent personality; in other words, he or she is a "pleaser." This type of person

- is unable to make everyday decisions without an excessive amount of advice or reassurance from others
- allows others to make most of his or her important decisions, e.g., where to live, what job to take
- agrees with people even when he or she believes they are wrong, because of fear of being rejected

- has difficulty initiating projects or doing things on his or her own
- volunteers to do things that are unpleasant or demeaning in order to get other people to like him or her
- feels uncomfortable or helpless when alone, or goes to great lengths to avoid being alone
- feels devastated or helpless when close relationships end
- is frequently preoccupied with fears of being abandoned
- is easily hurt by criticism or disapproval[10]

Cults excel in exploiting all types of personalities, but dependent pleasers seem to be a bit more over-represented in cult groups than in the rest of the population. Because pleasers are perhaps slightly more susceptible to being recruited, this does not mean they are to blame for becoming active in cults. They simply need education and support *before* cult association. If your child is a pleaser, there are things you can do to help cult-proof him or her.

Review this checklist and see a counselor if your child exhibits several of these behaviors. Next, encourage self-expression in your child by assertiveness training, social skills training, and just spending more time affirming him or her.

If your child is a dependent personality, the time to act is now in order to cult-proof them. Your child may always be a follower, and that is fine. Followers are people persons. But make that child aware that the need for approval and the fear of rejection are potentially dangerous snares that they must learn to overcome.

11
CULTS AND
THE CHURCH

There is an old saying to the effect that "the cults are the unpaid bills of the church." Elements of truth that have been neglected by the various Christian denominations have ... occasioned the rise of cults that unduly stressed such ignored or belittled truths to the point of creating a lopsided religion.
—J. K. Van Baalen in *The Chaos of the Cults*

What does your church teach about cults? Does your pastor, as so many pastors I have known, have little knowledge or interest in the subject of the cults? If your pastor does have a significant amount of knowledge on the cults, how often is this knowledge shared in the church in order to build up the expertise of the members?

The Reverend Richard L. Dowhower, a pastor in the Evangelical Lutheran Church in America, organizes conferences focusing on the cults. He told me that most pastors will not take seriously the plight of the cult victim unless they or someone in their family have been personally affected. In this regard, the cult problem is like the AIDS problem. Most pastors hold the view, "Certainly this is a problem, but it's not *my* problem." He also noted that most evangelicals get informed and involved in the cult problem only after losing a son or daughter to a cult. Finally, he observed that the church is so preoccupied with First Amendment issues that the cult problem more generally and the victims of cults more specifically are ignored. The typical pastor's mind-set is more on tolerance—a toleration of diversity in ideological perspective—than on carefully listening to the stories of victims.

Ronald Enroth, author of *Churches That Abuse*, agrees with Dowhower that pastors and the church in general have neglected the problem of cults. He told me, "I feel like telling them [pastors], 'You are a pastor, you have training. You should be able to do something about the cult problem.' They don't have the skills—even the bottom line stuff. You talk about apathy. It tends to be benign neglect, not purposeful. It's like cancer. They feel it won't happen until it happens, then they want help yesterday."

UNHELPFUL PASTORS

Parents frequently complain to me that their pastor is less than helpful and sometimes unsympathetic when it comes to their concerns about cults. Some pastors have even blamed parents for trying to get their child out of a cult! To test pastors, I sent parents of children at Wellspring a survey and asked them, "How did your pastor respond to your concerns about a cult problem?" Here are their replies:

- He didn't know what to do.
- He was not aware of the cult problem at all.
- He prayed with me but otherwise offered no directions.
- She told me not to worry about it, that my daughter would come around.

- I was more or less scolded for insinuating that a "doctrinally orthodox" group could in any way be dangerous.
- Our pastor talked with my daughter, but he did not understand how cults operate and control young people.
- He quietly listened but had nothing else to offer.
- The pastor told us to leave her alone and let her make her own decisions about the group and her religious affiliation.
- The pastor suggested that we see a psychologist or psychiatrist.
- Our pastor actually denied that the cult group even existed.

The parents and ex-cultists that I have surveyed rank advice from their pastors as follows: only ten percent said the advice was good. About thirty to forty percent thought that the pastor's advice was fair. And a full fifty percent rated their pastor's advice as poor!

When I shared the results of this informal survey with Harold Busséll, author of *Unholy Devotion: Why Cults Lure Christians*, he was not surprised. He sees so much abuse of authority within the ranks of evangelical pastors that he believes it makes them insensitive to the dangers of authoritarian cult groups. "Pastors can't take challenge to authority," he said. "It's a general tendency I see."

Christian pastors and other church leaders often do not know how to recognize cultic characteristics, and thus frequently unwittingly endorse or actually cooperate with some of these cultic organizations. The problem with some Christian leaders is that they have bought several of the "myths" about cults that we discussed earlier.

Much of the New Testament is given over to problems involving false teachers in the church—deceivers, false prophets, and "wolves in sheep's clothing." Scripture is not describing leaders who are "out there"—that is, overt non-Christians who can be spotted a mile away. The New Testament was clearly talking about leaders *within* the church—those professing to follow the true way of our Lord.

We can spot a "Bhagwan" type. Their teachings are strange, their dress quite different. But many Christians will miss the more clever deceiver—the person who dresses normally and seems to say all the right things. This "prophet" may appear even more dedicated than most pastors we know, more "on fire" for the Lord. He or she may have answers to those questions that always troubled you. Their church may be growing faster than your own. But this person is a false prophet.

LACK OF TEACHING ON THE CULTS

Denominations and churches are no better at combatting the cult problem. In a recent *Christianity Today* article entitled "The Kingdom of the Cult Watchers," Tim Stafford writes that there are over five hundred cult watch organizations, but only eight or nine of these have paid staff. Stafford points out that the Southern Baptists, Missouri Synod Lutherans, and Conservative Baptists were the only ones to offer anything in their seminaries on the new religions and the cults.[1]

Very few Bible schools, theological seminaries, or Christian colleges offer any significant teaching on cults. Of those institutions that do offer courses on cults, very few deal with the psychological dangers of these groups. Almost none teach about cultic *Christian* groups. And most classes limit their discussions to the theological heresies of the "classical" cults like Mormonism or Christian Science.

LACK OF MINISTRIES TO FORMER CULTISTS

Nor is the problem of treating ex-cultists handled any better by the Christian community, academic or otherwise. Few psychological or psychiatric facilities deal with ex-cultists, and only a handful of trained professional counselors specialize in treating these people.[2] Besides Wellspring Retreat and Resource Center, only one other rehabilitation center exists at the present time (though without a biblically or theologically trained staff). For those seeking help with cult-related spiritual or biblically-based problems, the options are appallingly few. To the best of my knowledge, aside from Wellspring there is no other professionally-staffed and theologically-trained residential facility in the world where former cultists can come for help in overcoming their cultic experience. Even aside from professional rehabilitation centers, there are only a handful of evangelically-oriented Christian counselors or psychologists who deal with former members on an out-patient basis. The clear point is that the lack of evangelical ministry to former cultists is appallingly inadequate, especially since those needing help are often themselves evangelical Christians!

WHAT IS THE CHURCH TRYING TO COMBAT?

Given the demonstrated apathy and the general ignorance of many pastors concerning the cult issue, especially on the psychological aspects of cultism, one must ask: What then *is* the church trying to combat?

It certainly does not appear to be cults. If the churches themselves or even their seminaries are teaching about and exposing cults on any large scale, it is a well-kept secret. It is fairly clear that most pastors have not been adequately sensitive to the cult problem. They probably don't realize that eighty percent of those now in cults were recruited from the pews of mainline and evangelical churches and synagogues.

Yet, what has the church done for those who suffer due to religious cults? I doubt if there are one hundred Christians in the world who devote full-time effort to cult rescue and research. As for cult rehabilitation, I know of none besides the work of Wellspring.

Charles Colson has properly chided the evangelical community for recent actions.[3] For example, in recent years the church has supported the Rev. Sun Myung Moon of the Unification Church in his tax-evasion case.[4] In fact, many Christians think that the United States government was simply out to get Moon. They reasoned that if the IRS was out to get Moon, eventually it would come after *us* and try to get us for tax-evasion. These Christians certainly did not agree with Moon's theology, but felt he was the target of a government meddling in the affairs of religious organizations. But Colson took another tack. He thought that Moon *deserved* what he got—and that our support for Moon was embarrassing.

Those of us in the anti-cult movement who agree with Colson have seen the government slow to do anything about Moon, or for that matter any other cults breaking the tax law and other laws. Moon has operated scores of businesses in the United States for many years, most of them little more than fronts for his Unification Church. Moon is not even a United States citizen, so for him to operate businesses in the United States, he must register with the government—something he has not done. Many have been aware of this fact and have protested to every known agency on Capitol Hill. Still no action has been taken, and Moon continues to operate his huge empire without even registering with the proper authorities. The *Frazier Report*, which was a congressional investigation into the Moon operation, recommended ways for the government to crack down on the Moon empire. But the *Frazier Report* is long forgotten, along with its recommendations.[5]

I do not suggest that we have a cavalier attitude about religious freedom. Religious freedom has often been something Christians have had to fight to defend. But if any religious organization does not live by the requirements of the law, then they should pay the price.

Christians should also be chided for siding with cults in lawsuits when victims have attempted to recover damages as a result of abuses suffered while members.[6] I find this defense incredible in light of biblical teaching to defend the widow, the orphan, the poor, and the homeless. Instead, the church has placed itself in the unbelievable position of defending the perpetrator—and blaming the victim.

When organizations such as The National Association of Evangelicals write "friend of the court" briefs on behalf of cultic organizations, it leaves the victim, who often professes Christianity, with a sense that somehow he is to blame for his unfortunate plight. What is the victim left to think? "If I were a better Christian this would not have happened to me." "What is wrong with me, that I am so wicked that I want to blame this organization and cause so much harm to it?" Or they may think, "If Christians won't help me out of this mess, then maybe the entire Christian faith is a lie. How could God allow this to happen?"

What is the church trying to combat? Evidently, the church has set its agenda on what it wants to fight.

Enemies of the Church

Evangelicals	*Liberals*
1. Pornography	1. Oppression of minorities
2. Abortion	2. Social injustice

3. Secular humanism
4. Drug and alcohol abuse
5. Immorality
6. Divorce
7. Declining religious freedom in public schools
8. Ignorance of the Gospel
9. Poverty

3. Hunger
4. Oppression of homosexuals
5. AIDS
6. Homelessness
7. Nuclear weapons
8. Discrimination against women
9. Poverty

Obviously these lists are incomplete and merely suggestive, and many of the issues are of great interest to both evangelicals and liberals. The point is that neither the liberal wing nor the evangelical wing of the church gives the cult issue priority.

CULTISTS SHOULD NOT BE TARGETS FOR EVANGELISM

As I have already stated, most cultists (eighty percent) are recruited from churches of the traditional Christian denominations. I have treated many ex-cultists who had made fully voluntary commitments to Christ prior or during their cultic experience. Remember Jim Jones and Jonestown? The 913 victims who died at the hands of this cult leader gone mad were our brothers and sisters—believers in Christ. They were normal people deceived by a cultic spiritual leader.

Many people active in the cults come from Christian backgrounds and made confessions of faith in Christ before joining these abusive groups. These Christians need to be restored and cared for. That is why I have said that Christians working in the cult field should not regard cultists primarily as targets for evangelism. They should not be evangelized, but *pastored*. People leaving cults are vulnerable. They need time for their critical thinking faculties to return to full functioning. Evangelism prior to the cultist's full recovery is an exploitation of vulnerabilities. Our primary ethical and Christian responsibility is to minister to them by offering information about cult dynamics, mind control, and cultic influence techniques. We must also be able to refer victims to counseling-support groups.

HEALTHY CHURCHES TEACH DOCTRINE

Christians often think that intense spiritual commitment is more important than one's doctrines or beliefs. But doctrines are sometimes incongruent with what goes on emotionally. In other words, while we may feel that what we do or believe is true and right, and even "Spirit-directed," these feelings may have nothing at all to do with the "truth." A pastor had a strong feeling that the Lord told him to divorce his wife and marry another woman in his congregation. Was he Spirit-directed? Obviously not.

Truth for many boils down to simple taste and preference. But we are not to base our life choices on our emotions. Rather, we are to base what we do on the teaching of Scripture.

Parents and churches, therefore, should teach doctrine—what we believe about God, humans, sin, salvation, the Bible, and future events—to children in such a way that it is clearly understood and made a part of their lives.

A clear understanding of the basic Gospel is essential. Cultic groups, whether coming from a Christian tradition or not, all uniformly distort and pervert the Gospel of God's grace in Christ. This perversion of the Christian message has become routine in these groups to which evangelicals fall prey. Why? Because we hold on to our faith in all the wrong places. For example, we confuse the message of the Gospel with our response to it. The Gospel becomes our "testimony"—what God has done for *me*. But in truth, the

Gospel is the historic message of Christ's life, death, and resurrection, and his atonement for the sins of the world.

After hearing the message of the Gospel, some people say things like, "Oh that sounds too easy—there must be something *more* to it." But there isn't. God justifies all of us by grace through simple, childlike faith. But the cults want us to think that this is just too simple, that something *more* is needed. We need to teach our kids to hold on to their faith in all the *right* places.

Gordon Lewis of Denver Seminary said, "We have heard so much from our devotional writers that it's more important to experience God than to define him. We must explode the view that any spiritual experience is good. If Satan is a deceiver who disguises himself as an angel of light, it can be suicide to expose yourself to any spiritual experience that comes along. It will be tragic if creeds do not become important to the church again."[7]

Writer Tim Stafford agrees. "You would have to look hard to find much excitement about doctrine," he writes. "But for how much longer?"[8]

That is my cry. How much longer will the church neglect its core teachings? How much longer will she ignore the problems caused by false prophets and teachers? I pray it will not be long. As the late Walter Martin writes:

> Never before in religious history have so many people become so rapidly aware of the dangers of cultism. . . . New cults constitute a serious threat in many areas, not only to their own physical well-being and spiritual well-being, but to the Christian church as well. Many of these cults prey on the young and the uninformed, and we ignore them only at great risk to ourselves and our church.[9]

12

CULTS AND SOCIETY

There's always a pretty good number of self-appointed pied pipers, self-appointed messianic people, self-appointed gurus in any society who say to the confused masses: "Follow me! I have a simple solution for the complex problems of life." But if the social structure has not broken down, very few people will follow them.

—Dr. Margaret Thaler Singer
in *Cults and Consequences*

Horror stories about cults abound. In some cults, members were told it was a sin to sleep more than three to four hours per day. In other groups, the leaders wanted donations in cash only so that the IRS couldn't trace them. Many ex-members of various cultic groups were told that they would go to hell or become possessed by demons if they left the group. I could give hundreds of other examples to show that most cults are dangerous—and they hurt people.

Then why is it that so many people join cults? The

answer to that question lies not only in the individual needs we all have. There are also *societal* causes for the proliferation of cults. The underlying beliefs—or world-view—of most Americans contribute to their susceptibility to cults.

FALSE BELIEFS

Most of us are looking for security because we sense that our society is crumbling around us. Things are in such a constant state of flux that we feel insecure, confused, and lonely. We are bothered by AIDS, crime, rape, the threat of nuclear war, divorce, the unemployment figures, inflation, pollution, war, the loss of our roots, and the crumbling of the family. Our insecurity is often caused by false beliefs, which leave us open to the influence of cults.

False Belief #1: Life Is Simple

In the midst of confusion and despair, the media constantly tries to convince us that there are simple answers. For example, a TV movie depicts a troubled family that is suddenly "fixed" when the daughter confronts her father. Dad cries, they hug, and promise to spend more time together. The credits roll.

National network news portrays a world crisis in two minutes as though the crisis started five minutes prior to broadcast. Two "experts" invariably give their opinions, and usually these opinions are contrary to our government's official policy. We get the impression that a few "experts" could solve the crisis in a few minutes if only someone would give them the chance.

Easy answers are offered in virtually every field. Look at the books in the stores with titles like *The Five Minute Manager* or *Get Rich in 30 Days*. Modern society gives us simple answers to complex questions.

Cults do the same. They prey on our tendency to look for simple answers and our desire to label things as either all black or all white. Often our own search for the easy way out is an excuse for refusing to think and use our own minds.

Adolf Hitler said, "What good fortune for leaders that men do not think." The unscrupulous make easy prey of the mindless. The tragic results can be witnessed in history with all the victims who have fallen prey to the likes of Hitler. The same mechanisms used to reduce people to following a Hitler operate in cults in this country as well.

False Belief #2: Success Is Everything

Nearly all television commercials portray the powerful images of success, prosperity, youth, and good looks. Most Americans devote their entire lives to being successful. For most of us, the road to "success" is elusive and difficult. Promises of an easier road or a surer method will grab our attention. I believe this is why cults so often package themselves as "ways to success."

In fact, many cults are blatantly success-oriented. Many cult-operated management training courses and professional seminars on self-improvement are mere gimmicks to separate you from your money and attack your concept of self worth. They do not deliver what they promise.[1]

Sadly, our success-oriented society makes it very easy for religious hucksters to market their wares in the form of spiritual success and material prosperity as ordained by God. But the only ones who seem to be reaping dividends are the types of leaders who say, "Give your tithe to God (i.e., my ministry) and he will bless you." God blesses in his own way, whether we give to a particular ministry or not. The Bible does not promise material blessing to people who are faithful, even though many fringe Christian leaders teach that obedience and faith are absolute guarantees for success and prosperity.

But Jesus was homeless and he had little if any money. He said, "Foxes have holes and birds of the air have nests, but the Son of Man has no place to lay his head" (Luke 9:58). The life of dedication and service to God is no guarantee of prosperity or material blessing. Jesus died a poor man.

Paul was often shipwrecked, hungry, cold, penniless, and poorly clothed. Yet he was an apostle of Christ who became the church's obedient servant and did not often receive any material blessing. Paul's entire life was devoted to preaching and traveling—hardly the way to build riches.

Many others in Scripture lived righteous lives and yet were not wealthy. Nevertheless, one of the fastest-growing movements in the church today centers on the so-called "prosperity teaching" or "positive confession" doctrine, declaring that material prosperity and physical health can be "claimed" by all Christians who confess in faith the desire for health and prosperity and then believe they will receive it. These Christians who hold to this "prosperity teaching" may even blame the starving and poor for their own lack of positive confession.[2] However, as Martin Luther noted, true preachers of the gospel are always suffering hardship and the wealth of other preachers is due not to their faith but to their false and enticing doctrine.[3]

Life is not simple and success is not everything. As Solomon noted:

> The race is not to the swift
>   or the battle to the strong,
> nor does food come to the wise
>   or wealth to the brilliant
>   or favor to the learned;
> but time and chance happen to them all.

Moreover, no man knows when his hour will come:
As fish are caught in a cruel net,
    or birds are taken in a snare,
so men are trapped by evil times
    that fall unexpectedly upon them.

(Eccl. 9:11–12)

False Belief #3: We Must Change in Order to Belong

Like success, the desire to belong can be a trap for the unwary. What price must be paid to be accepted? What type of people require outsiders to change before they are accepted? What type of change does God want before he accepts us?

Much of what our society and, unfortunately, some of what our churches teach us about change is plain balderdash. I have counseled countless Christians who said they were taught that they had to do this or that and then God maybe, just maybe, would accept them. We carry this same unfortunate mindset into our everyday relationships with friends, parents, and spouses. But that is not grace. Biblical grace is an acceptance based on nothing we have done or can do to make ourselves worthy.

We all need to belong and to cover the emptiness inside us. We may have grown up in a home where we were not affirmed or where affirmation was very conditional. I have often heard my clients say that they could never please their mother, or that whatever they did, it was never good enough for their father. Kids raised with a lack of acceptance at home, at church, or in school will search to be fulfilled in other ways. Cultic or aberrational groups promise that God will fill the void in their heart and that he will do it through their group. But the cults and fringe churches don't deliver on their promise.

False Belief #4: Efficiency is the Greatest Good

Jacques Ellul, a French sociologist who has written widely on the perils of modern society and the shortcomings of the church, has pointed out the damaging effects of an emphasis on efficiency at all costs. Efficient work can be dehumanizing. Companies may fire workers if there is a more efficient way to do things. A new machine may make a worker's job easier and more efficient, but job stress may rise due to higher quotas. Entire countries may base their major political and economic decisions on efficiency. Stalinist Russia liquidated enemies as a more efficient way of handling problems.

Ellul argues that it may not always be the most moral thing to get things done quickly and efficiently. Speed and efficiency, he says, have little to do with the human spirit. There is a natural God-ordained rhythm to life that our modern society has drowned out, and God values other things besides efficiency.

I bring this up because the problem of efficiency is especially prominent in cults. In these groups, the chief good is "fruit," "numbers," "growth," and "size." Somehow, many religiously-oriented cults equate spirituality and blessing with efficiency, or with results. We must beware, and teach our children to beware, of the seduction of "technique." "Scientific" methods of efficiency can destroy the vibrancy of the human spirit and rob God of his majesty.

Currently the nation of Japan illustrates efficiency and production at their most awesome. The Japanese are fast becoming the world leaders in automobile manufacturing, real estate, banking, and computer and high-tech electronics. But we also hear of the "Fatal Burnout Syndrome" that increasingly afflicts the Japanese work force. Their workers literally are dying from overwork.[4]

How can we avoid the ill effects on the human spirit of ruthless efficiency?

We have to try hard to match each person's needs and talents with appropriate tasks and the means to accomplish them. We must urge our leaders to become more sensitive to individual needs, and to realize what grave dangers can be inflicted by leaders who supposedly speak for God and make unlimited demands on those who answer to them. We must be like Jacob, who realized that if he drove his flocks or his children hard for one day they were in danger of perishing (Gen. 33:13–14). Wisdom and ethics dictate that the pace be determined by the capacity of the individual person and not by efficiency.

Why not offer people the freedom in ministry to create their own jobs and freely choose their own areas of interest? A number of churches and ministries work very hard to develop the gifts and talents of their members. Over the years Francis Schaeffer's L'Abri ministry in Switzerland has devoted considerable effort to reinforcing the artistic talents and abilities of young Christians. In our counseling at Wellspring we explore with our clients their personality type, gifts, and talents, and try to show them how to develop their unique abilities. Parents should sensitize themselves and their children to look for churches and ministries that allow them this kind of freedom.

Stressing a "kinder and gentler" view of Christian work and mission would be another point. My brother graduated from an evangelical seminary in this country. Steve was not afraid of hard work. But at one point during the course of his seminary studies he went to the dean and politely complained that the work load seemed unreasonably demanding. Steve found no time for anything besides seminary work, and he reminded the dean that even Jesus attempted to give his disciples time to rest. Steve knew that the pastorate was demanding and tough, and that seminary students had to be prepared for great stress. But he feared that the training was so rigorous that some would quit before they even entered the pastorate. Could this type of training contribute to burnout among theological students?

The dean told my brother, "Well, Steve, that's just the way it is." A few weeks later the dean was found in his office at home, slumped over his typewriter. He was dead of a heart attack.

The pressure that seminary professors live under may well be transferred to the seminary *student*, who in turn transfers it to his or her future congregation. I have probably heard five hundred sermons about how uncommitted we are for every single sermon I have heard about the need to slow down, relax, and enjoy God, one's family, and life in general.

Regular church-goers have become so conditioned to messages about dedication that for some any new twist on dedication becomes the hook necessary to lure them into an aberrational Christian movement. Cults will always find deficiencies within the church and call it "lukewarm." But for the cults, the difference between being "hot" and being "lukewarm" leads to only one thing—a type of fanatical, elitist mentality that can drive many to total physical and mental collapse. To be "hot" does not mean to be excessive in our zeal. One can be "kinder and gentler" and still avoid being lukewarm.

The Bible itself points out pitfalls of misguided dedication. Paul spoke of some Jews who had a zeal for God that was devoid of correct knowledge (Rom. 10:2). Even longer ago, Solomon warned of misguided dedication: "Do not be overrighteous, neither be overwise—why destroy yourself?"(Eccl. 7:16). Dedication to God is not based on a performance model but on grace working through faith. It is quite possible that we may actually accomplish more spiritual good by doing less.

Burnout exists in Christian vocations as well as in secular employment, and its denial is a corollary of the proposition that efficiency and "fruit" are our highest moral goals. The church needs to develop a theology of burnout and take appropriate steps to recognize it, prevent it, and treat it should it occur. This is one reason the church is blinded by the errors of cultism. Cults are very dedicated. They work hard and they can be extraordinarily efficient.

To many people, the philosophy of the church can be expressed in such slogans as:

- "It's better to burn out than to rust out."
- "Every moment counts for eternity."
- "Work while it is yet day."
- "Redeem the time."
- "Don't settle for God's second best."

Too many Christian young people have been pre-programmed by these slogans, making them even more vulnerable to cultic groups that exploit the idea of working for God's kingdom. Living in this kind of high pressure results in a chronic state of stress. The irony is that once this stress shows up to the point that the Christian worker is affected, that worker is viewed as spiritually unfit. We will all succumb to stress in our Christian lives if our activity is not balanced by proper rest, exercise, support, and recreation.

OTHER CULTURAL PHENOMENA

Besides false beliefs, there are other cultural phenomena that contribute to and explain the proliferation of cults, including the wide use of drugs, the popularity of rock music, and the rise of Satanism and the occult.

The Wide Use of Drugs

As with cults, drugs are symptomatic of a deeper sickness within society. If anything marks our technologically oriented society, it is change. For many, change has meant a feeling of helplessness. They feel their efforts and ideas will have no bearing on where society is heading. Change and our inability to control it has contributed to a loss of self-identity and feelings of alienation.

Our society promotes a value system that contains within itself its own seeds of self-destruction. This value system promotes feelings, experiences, and tolerance over such things as truth, honesty, and justice. We take drugs because it feels good, and because it is good to feel good. And many of our children join cults, or some off-base Christian groups, because it makes them feel good in many ways.

Our society has produced numerous persons who do not accept or love themselves. This creates a void that they try to fill in a number of ways. Many try drugs or alcohol, and others who don't fall for these addictions fill the void in more socially acceptable ways—shopping, spending, or workaholism. For many Christians, this void is filled by ministry, or by helping others.

People do not stop using drugs or recover completely from cults until they fill the void with healthy self-love—not selfishness or pride, but a recognition of their own worth. People without self-love will eventually destroy themselves in one way or another, through one addiction or another, trying endlessly to find something to make them feel good about themselves, and to make them feel loved.

The Popularity of Rock Music

Increasingly, a larger segment of our society, Christians and non-Christians alike, are realizing the dangers of modern music. Heavy metal music clearly offers a message of lust, hatred, blood, murder, suicide, and destruction. Tipper Gore and a group of concerned mothers have done an excellent job of exposing the dangers of heavy metal music and how it easily skirts pornography restrictions that would apply to equivalent messages in print.[5]

In his live act, Alice Cooper uses a guillotine to sever the head of a mannequin. He advises those in the first few rows to wear blood bibs, or rain coats.[6] Cooper sings of making love to dead women; the Dead Kennedys sing of poisoning and killing little children; the group Vanity sings of constant sexual climax; and Motley Crue makes lewd remarks about female genitals during their performances. There are nearly endless examples of sex, violence, and Satanism in the heavy metal rock music field.

Allan Bloom, in his book *The Closing of the American Mind*, offers this sweeping judgment of the effects of rock music:

> Picture a thirteen-year-old boy sitting in the living room of his family home doing his math assignment while wearing his Walkman headphones or watching MTV. He enjoys the liberties hard won over centuries by the alliance of philosophic genius and political heroism, consecrated by the blood of martyrs; he is provided with comfort and leisure by the most productive economy ever known to mankind; science has penetrated the secrets of nature in order to provide him with the marvelous, lifelike electronic sound and image reproduction he is enjoying. And in what does progress culminate? A pubescent child whose body throbs with orgasmic rhythms; whose feelings are made articulate in hymns to the joys of onanism or the killing of parents; whose ambition is to win fame and wealth in imitating the drag-queen who makes the music. In short, life is made into a nonstop, commercially prepackaged masturbational fantasy.[7]

The rebellion produced by rock music-inspired youth is producing an authentic revolution in society—a revolution of selfishness and instant gratification. As rock music encourages kids to rebel against parents, this rebellion spreads to *anything* restricting wanton self-desires.

The Rise of Satanism and the Occult

How did our society travel the path from the hippie revolution to the drug culture, and then to heavy metal music and to occultism? The answer is in the nature of society itself. Sweeping technological changes, along with the erosion of our civilized structures such as family and church, have created a sense of loneliness, helplessness, and alienation in our young people. For some, turning to drugs, heavy metal music, or to cults seems to fill this void. But for others, the void is filled only by something more powerful, more gruesome. And so they turn to the occult, and to violence, for in these they find the experiences they are looking for. For a few of these people it involves a deliberate choice of evil, for they are not deceived into thinking what they are doing is good—as in the case of many cultists. In the case of violent occultism and Satanism, evil becomes the good. And they willingly choose this "new" good.

Even Christians are caught up in this fascination with Satanism. They will buy books and attend seminars on Satanism, but neglect to learn or do anything about cults. Like the general population, Christians seem to be caught up in a perverse desire to be shocked and entertained.

CONCLUSION

Christians are not exempt from being influenced by their culture. To cult-proof our kids, therefore, we need to be aware of and opposed to all the false beliefs and cultural influences that would pull us away from the truth and toward a cult.

RECOVERY FROM CULT INVOLVEMENT

13
WHEN YOUR CHILD JOINS A CULT

To have someone you love in a cult is like a living death. I compare it to the grief of watching a person die knowing there is a cure and being unable to use it.
—Henrietta Crampton in *Cults and Consequences*

Dorothy Wishmeyer and her husband George worshipped in a sound evangelical church. All three of their children were active in the church, and their daughter, Carolyn, was attending a university offering one of the best music programs in the country. While away at college, Carolyn found a tremendous group of Christians who were loving and on fire for the Lord. Carolyn had always loved the Lord and was a deeply committed Christian. But gradually her personality changed. Her contact with her parents decreased, and she grew critical of her home church.

Mrs. Wishmeyer suspected something was "cultic" about the group in which Carolyn was involved—the Boston Church of Christ. I was able to confirm her suspicions. When she asked what she and her husband could do, I gave her the following advice.

DON'T PANIC

It is not always so easy to find information about a group. A common tendency is to panic in the absence of data. Don't panic and jump to conclusions. What is your evidence that a group is cultic? Here are a few practical guidelines and suggestions to help you work through this troubling problem. Begin by asking some questions about changes in your child's personality and behavior patterns.

1. Has your contact with your child decreased in recent weeks or months? Has communicating with your child become more difficult?
2. Have you recently observed an increased hostility in your child?
3. Has your child seemingly lost his or her sense of humor?
4. Does your child appear more serious?
5. If in school, have your child's grades dramatically dropped?
6. Have you noticed a sudden change in your son or daughter's dating or friendships?
7. Does he or she spend a lot of time with a new group or religious organization?
8. Are you being preached at as though you need to be "saved"?
9. Has there been a dramatic change in your child's career interest—or in her place of residence?
10. Does your child have a glassy stare in her eyes, or does she seem "spaced out" or not quite there?

If you answered "yes" to most of these questions, you may want to seriously consider that your child may be involved in drug use, that she is in some sort of troubling or threatening situation, that she is ill, or that she has become involved in some cultic activity. If you suspect involvement in a cult, what do you do next?

STEPS TO TAKE IN A CULT CRISIS

Find Someone to Talk To

In the middle of a crisis that concerns your child, you quite possibly and even reasonably can become so focused on the crisis that you may lose touch with your own feelings. Anxiety, worry, anger, and guilt feelings may cause panic.

Talk to a close friend, to your pastor, or to a professional counselor. Find someone who can validate your feelings. It will do you no good for someone to reject or trivialize your feelings by telling you that you shouldn't be feeling the way you feel, or that it is wrong to feel anger and guilt, or that you couldn't possibly be worried about anything. Instead, find a caring listener who is able to affirm you in what you are going through, someone who can understand that you are nervous and worried about your child.

It is crucial to explore your feelings. Have someone validate those feelings to help you come to grips with the fact that you are feeling upset, angry, depressed—or any of a host of other emotions that become all mixed together at times. Anyone who minimizes your feelings does two things. To begin with, they offer a false picture of how much the problem affects you. An effective listener or counselor will help you see how worry over the cultic involvement of your loved one has taken control of your life and lessened your ability to act and to help your child. This principle is the same one that is used when family members intervene to get alcoholic sons, daughters, or other family members into treatment.[1]

Those who minimize your feelings are also stripping away the very thing that is crucial for a successful intervention, namely sharing your feelings with the person in the cult. Again, as with successful interventions in alcoholism, your feelings are certainly the most powerful tool to stop the one you love from destroying himself in a cult.

Develop a checklist of your feelings in order to assess how anxious, depressed, and worried you have become. When you begin to see how much of each day is being taken over with thoughts and questions about your child, the more motivated you will be to take the next step and educate yourself about the cults.

Educate Yourself About the Cults

Now you and your support person—whether a friend, pastor, or counselor—can begin to gather information about the particular group that your son or daughter has joined. You may wish to read certain books on the destructive nature of cults, like Steve Hassan's *Combatting Cult Mind Control*. Check what you know about the group in question with the criteria for a destructive group. If you are convinced that there have been personality changes in your child and that these changes have something to do with their cultic involvement, then continue to do some further research.

Gather Information

Step 1

Call or write to the following and ask them is they have any information on the particular group or the leader of the group. Request that they send you any information they may have. All of these groups and others are listed with phone numbers and addresses in Appendix A in this book.

- Cult Awareness Network
- American Family Foundation
- Christian Research Institute

- Watchman Fellowship
- Personal Freedom Outreach
- Other organizations listed in Appendix A.

Step 2

Whether or not you obtained any information from Step 1, continue your research by phoning as many other authorities as possible from the following list:

- The local police or sheriff's office in the town where your child's group is located. Here are some matters you should cover.
  1. Ask if they have ever heard of or dealt with the group. (Be specific. Name the group and ask the police if they have had any complaints about it. Be aware, however, that the group may go by several names, so give all names if you know them.)
  2. Ask if they have come in contact with or heard about the group's leader. Ask if there have been any complaints against him or her.
  3. Inquire if they have had complaints about other key figures in the group that your child may have mentioned.
  4. Ask the officer to be as specific as possible about the types of inquiries or complaints. If they provide you with names of former members, talk to those people, but be careful and courteous, and just gather information.
  5. Be prepared to give your name. If you don't want to give your name, have a friend call for you.
  6. If you have come up empty at this point, don't worry. It is quite possible that the authorities have not heard anything or have had no contact with the group you are trying to assess. Continue your investigation anyway.

Check the following sources:

- Local newspapers, radio and television stations, to see if any articles, reports, or investigations have been done regarding the group.
- The local ministerial association or individual local pastors, to obtain any information they may have.
- The Dean of Students office, if your child was recruited by the group on a college campus.
- The local mental health center. Ask for general information to see if anyone sought services there as a result of being in the group.

In addition:

- Ask your child for literature from the group. Simply tell him or her that you are interested in learning more about them.
- Check with a librarian to see if there are any newspaper or magazine articles on the ministry or its leader.
- Visit the group. Meet the members and the leaders and gather information. Ask hard questions, but be friendly and polite.

Step 3

Evaluate the data. Determine if the church or ministry is or is not aberrant from a traditional Christian point of view. Do not label any group a "cult" unless you are sure that it is. Recheck the facts. Compare your findings with the criteria for a cult listed in the first chapter of this book. Don't go on a witch hunt and prematurely judge a group to be either cultic or dangerous. Review whatever evidence you have gathered with your pastor or a close friend. Do they agree with your conclusion?

Remember, you could be wrong. What accounts for

the personality change in your child if the group in which she is involved is not in fact a cult? Perhaps there was a noncoercive conversion. Just because your child has become active in a different type of religious group doesn't mean that it is a cult in the psychological sense. There may be absolutely no evidence that any undue influence or psychological coercion was used to attract the young person to the particular group. A change from a noncharismatic to a charismatic form of worship, or vice versa, may be disturbing to some Christian parents, but it may just show that your child prefers another emphasis or style when it comes to church attendance or worship. It hardly offers any proof of cultism. In the same vein, your child may experiment with Eastern meditation, Buddhism, yoga, or any number of non-Christian and non-Western traditions. This may be a heart-wrenching experience for Christian parents, and it certainly calls for some frank and open family communication, but it doesn't mean that your child is beyond rescue because they have fallen into a cult. Membership in an alternative religious community is not necessarily a sign that coercive forces are operating.

If you have completed the research and information gathering and have no clear evidence that your child is in a destructive group, my advice is to wait and see. Continue to monitor the situation and check for signals of aberrant behavior. Have a heart-to-heart discussion with your son or daughter. Let them know, without attacking either them or their group, of your observations of the group, the changes in their behavior, and your love and concern for them.

It is important not to accuse or confront your child.[2] When you confront people, as a rule they become defensive and close off conversation. Keep negative comments to a minimum. They skirt the real issue of how the cultic involvement has affected the family, and produced changes in the family member. Try to improve family communications, instead of creating a further barrier with your child. It is best to avoid the suggestion of brainwashing, as well as criticism of the leadership of the particular group. Almost invariably when a parent argues with a child over that child's beliefs, the two-way conversation closes down—so avoid doing this as well.

Instead, maintain an interest in the activities your son or daughter pursues. Reaffirm your approval of their good actions, motives, and intentions (but do not give express approval of the group). Attend group activities or church together (but don't go to retreats or long seminars sponsored by the group in question). Try some negotiation: Go to a worship service or Bible study with your child if they will give you equal time in the future.

What to Do When Your Child Has Joined a Cult

There are some general yet essential things you must do if and when you discover that your son or daughter belongs to a cult.

1. Take your time. Don't rush or panic.
2. Continue to educate yourself about cults and especially about the particular group your child has joined.
3. Talk to other parents who have a family member in a cult. What have they done to help or minister to that person?
4. Try to locate former members of the group in which your child is involved. Talk with them and learn as much as you can about the reasons people join and leave the group.

By now your information has been gathered, and you have shared the results with a trusted friend or professional, such as your pastor. And by now you are probably so concerned about your son or daughter that you may have lost track of your own feelings of guilt, shame, panic, anger at God, rejection, and hurt. You plainly feel misunderstood. I advised you to be aware of your feelings at the beginning of your research. It is equally important now to come to terms with your feelings.

Often parents blame themselves for their child's involvement in aberrational associations. Perhaps if we had only loved our son more, they reason, or paid more attention to our daughter's new group of friends, they would not have joined. It is natural and normal to feel this way. There is no question that we all could and should have done things differently in rearing our children. But second-guessing is an endless game where participants lose every time. Parents are never perfect. Most of the facts show that parents are not to blame for their child's cult experience. We are not all-wise and all-powerful, and we can no more control our child's ultimate destiny regarding cults than we can determine most other aspects of their lives. But that does not mean we are helpless. There are things we can do.

Parents should not feel guilty, though many will feel rejected. They may be angry at their child for joining a cult, summarily dismissing them from their lives. And for the devoted cultist, this is fine. Cults teach directly or indirectly that members should purposefully withdraw from parents because they are "threats" to the mission of the group. If the child is a thoroughly loyal devotee, inevitably there will be less and less contact and intimacy with parents. Therefore, it is the inbuilt cult dynamic that is responsible for the ruptured relationships and not the child's deliberate attempt to hurt anyone.

It is also common for parents to be angry at God. "God, why did you take my son from me?" "Are you punishing us for some horrible sin we have not confessed?" These and other very troubling thoughts can intensify the crisis you are already in. Remember that many parents have had such thoughts. It will do no good to deny your anger—all of us at times are troubled by the suffering and unexpected difficulties in our lives and the lives of our loved ones. Only occasionally do we ever get a rational or logical answer to "why?" We are only finite and see things from a limited perspective. This is all to say that a child in a cult can be a serious trial of faith for parents. By faith parents can begin to see that God ultimately is in control, and in all things he works for the good of those who love him (Rom. 8:28). Merely reciting Scripture verses will not solve the problem, however. Renewal of faith is nourished in the furnace of suffering. At these times, faithful and understanding friends and counselors can provide the support we need.

Develop and Implement a Plan for Intervention

Once you have a handle on your feelings of rejection and grief, you can begin more effectively to formulate a plan for helping your child or loved one exit the cult. Actually, an intervention for a cult member can be very similar to interventions used in attempting to get an alcoholic or drug-addicted family member into professional treatment. This is how an expert in the field of alcoholism interventions defines the process: It is

> a move initiated out of love and concern by the people who care about the alcoholic. It involves their getting together to tell the alcoholic the facts about his disease and how it is affecting them. It's the only kind, gentle, and caring way to help a chemically dependent person. It's the only thing that works, the key to stopping someone whose life is in danger.
>
> Today the term "intervention" refers to a carefully constructed and orchestrated process in which the family, friends, and perhaps an employer talk to the

alcoholic or drug user. Trained counselors prepare the concerned parties, educating them about alcoholism as a disease, guiding them to collect their thoughts, giving them reassurance, and preparing them for everything and anything that might happen during intervention. The objective is to make the alcoholic agree to have professional evaluation or enter into treatment.[3]

An intervention with a cultist must be motivated out of the love of concerned family members or others close to the individual. The purpose of such an orchestrated process is to educate the cult member about the dynamics of controlling groups. The intervention will detail how involvement with a particular group has affected both the group member and the other members of the family. The goal is to encourage the person to reevaluate his participation, or, in severe cases, to get him into treatment. The goal of such intervention is never to force or coerce your loved one to admit that he or she is in a cult.

In my opinion, the best approach in intervention is to work with people with experience and an established reputation in helping people leave cults. Pastors, mental health professionals, or professional "exit counselors" who conduct interventions with cultists in an effort to convince them to leave their group, can be consulted. Professional exit counselors have specialized training and expertise in conducting these sorts of interventions. They are *not* "deprogrammers." Exit counselors do not detain people against their will, nor do they recommend forced removal from the group. Persuasion is done indirectly, and almost exclusively by talk. Family members play a big role by sharing their feelings about how the cult has affected them. People are moved by feelings, and cult members are no exception. Most interventions enable one to see the care and the love that the family has for them. Interventions also use the showing of testimonial videos, documentaries, or talk shows dealing with the cultist's particular group or similar ones. Reading material is also provided for the member to learn what the news media or religious and mental health professionals have written about the group in question. The exit counselor also shares information about the dynamics of controlling groups in general, and about some of the specifics of the particular group that the person may not know. Experts in the field can be contacted through the organizations listed in Step 1 earlier in this chapter.

Do not hire someone who recommends kidnapping your child or holding him against his will. Avoid them like the plague. Kidnapping is an illegal act, and if they fail to deliver your child, legal action may be taken against you by your child or by the cult. If the case against you is strong, you could possibly serve time in prison; even if you are not convicted, you will most likely have done irrevocable damage to the relationship with your child.

If your child is subject to physical or psychological harm, or has possibly been made to participate in illegal activities, then by all means contact a lawyer who knows about cult-related issues and seek his or her advice. A number of lawyers can be contacted through the American Family Foundation (P.O. Box 336, Weston, MA 02193) and the Cult Awareness Network (2421 West Pratt Blvd. Suite 1173, Chicago, IL 60645).

If you decide to hire an expert on cults, such as an exit counselor, here are some of the things you should typically expect from them.

What Professional Cult Experts Will Do

In the book *Exit Counseling,* Carol Giambalvo gives the following eighteen points that explain what professional cult experts will do if you hire them to help you with your child.[4]

1. Counselors will first consult with you and continue to resolve any fear or panic you have regarding your child or loved one.
2. They will offer guidelines on how to handle the cult member prior to any intervention.
3. They will gather some basic information about your family, your child, and the nature of the cult group. The counselor will want detailed information specifically about your child's role in the cult.
4. They will discuss their fees and expenses with you.
5. They will need to know about any family problems with drug or alcohol abuse, prior conflicts between parents and the child, and mental health matters. If significant family problems are evident, most counselors will consult a mental health professional about the feasibility of a direct intervention, the timing of such an intervention, or the recommendation of the presence of a mental health professional during the actual exit counseling process.
6. They will encourage you to consult books and other reading materials on cults. Knowledge of thought reform techniques is crucial in helping parents understand how their child was recruited and retained in the cult.
7. Exit counselors will try to give parents information about the group by getting them in contact with former members of the cult. This will help educate parents about the cult and give them a greater sense of control.
8. Reputable exit counselors will provide references upon request.
9. The counselor will offer advice about the timing and location of the intervention, and who should be in-

volved in the intervention team. Timing is usually determined by various calendar events that would normally bring a family member home, such as vacations, holidays, birthdays, and so on. Usually it will not help to deceive anyone. The counselor will probably advise you to say something along these lines: "We have to have a family discussion that will involve every member of the family. I have been getting some counsel for myself, and I would like you to come to this discussion."[5]

10. The logistics of travel arrangements for the team, where they will stay, and the daily schedule, including breaks, will be discussed fully before any plan is finalized.

11. The length (usually three to five days) and the nature of intervention are fully discussed with the family ahead of time. The intervention itself normally consists of the following steps that are consistent with interventions used in helping both drug and alcohol addicts:

- Getting the person to the intervention site.
- Setting up the logistics and conditions—the place, rules of conduct for team members, how to handle the phone, the doorbell, and other things.
- Deciding who will be the first person to speak and what this person will say. Generally, the counselor will mention that he has been working with the family and that he is there to talk about the group the person has been involved with.
- Requesting that the person listen. At this point it is premature to suggest that the person change her point of view or seek help.
- Sharing carefully thought-out notes on how the cult participation has affected the family by each

person who knows about or who has been affected by the member's cultic involvement. Here is an example of what one mother said to her son:

"Josh, I'm sharing these thoughts because I love you. I suffered greatly during the process of giving birth to you. And I know that God has blessed me in allowing me to be your mother. But Josh, your involvement with this group has given me more pain than I could ever dream possible. I feel that I'm losing you. Our entire family is in anguish over you. You are spending more and more time with your friends in this new group and almost no time at home. You didn't come home for your birthday. You knew we were planning a big party. And then you didn't even come to your sister's wedding. You acted like it was no big deal. For a while I was very angry and hurt over what you have done. But I must set my feelings aside for now. I must be concerned about you. You are not yourself anymore. You don't look, talk, or act the same. Something else is controlling you. And I can only say that you are cutting yourself off from the people who love you. You are hurting yourself, Josh. As I get older, I want my son. I want to see you graduate, marry, find a job, and have a family. I want to be a part of that, but you are gone. You are like a stranger to me. Please, listen to what we have to say."

• Preparing for other contingencies—keeping people on task, knowing all the details of the intervention and making plans ahead of time for further treatment if this is agreed upon, preparing the team for the rare instance of the person leaving during the process of the intervention, and sticking to the decision to accept the consequences even if the cult member refuses to listen and decides to return to the cult.[6]

12. Professional cult experts will discuss issues of confidentiality with the family ahead of time. This includes who will be on the intervention team, and deciding who *not* to inform about the intervention. Generally it is best for the group member not to know about the specific details of the intervention, or even to know about how informed the parents are about the group.

13. Prior to the intervention, the exit counselor will encourage each family member, friend, or other significant person on the team to talk about their feelings and concerns.

    Each member on the intervention team will be coached on exactly what to say to the client, and therefore some role-playing of possible scenarios may be done.

14. The exit counselor will fully inform the parents about the possible reactions to the intervention. Clients are typically angry at these interventions. They may accuse parents of being tools of Satan. They may feel tricked, if the intervention was a surprise to them. All team members should be prepared for such responses, and consequently they need to fully settle in their own minds why such an intervention is necessary. Would the cult leader have granted permission for the child to hear contrary information? If the cult member had learned about the intervention, would the cult leader's advice have been sought? Would he or she have agreed in advance to a fully voluntary dialogue about the cult?

Would other methods of intervention be as successful? What would be the risk to the family member to do nothing?

The client may refuse to listen. If that happens, there will be anger and vacillation before any significant breakthroughs are evident. It is therefore sometimes preferable for the parents or other significant family members of the team to present the plan for intervention to the cult member. If the member consents, then the rest of the team will be invited in. Even during the intervention the client will be told that he can leave whenever he wants. It is also advisable for the cult members to be assured very specifically that the intervention is in no way a challenge to their faith or belief in God. The intervention team is there simply to present information about the group that the cult member has not seen or heard, probably because it has been deliberately withheld or distorted by the group.

15. The intervention itself will be presented to the family as education, not therapy. The focus of exit counseling is to help people realize how the dynamics of powerful persuasion techniques can have an undue influence and result in a lack of any real clear informed consent about the nature of the participation in the group. Interventions allow family members and others close to the cult member to share fully their concern and their feelings about the person's involvement, and how it has affected them. The following is a brief summary of the methods and procedures used in the counseling process:

- Cult members are treated with dignity and respect. Face to face confrontations and yelling are not acts of respect, and they should not be tolerated.

- Materials presented during intervention will also include the positive aspects of the group. All information will be thoroughly reviewed and discussed.
- During the initial phase, the counselor will gather information on the member's attraction to the group, reasons why she joined, any doubts the member has had while in the group, what perceptions the person has now versus initial impressions, and what the client would be doing if not part of the group. This information will allow the exit counselor to determine the client's needs and help plan the next phase of intervention.
- Issues of manipulation, mind control, and accusations others have made against the group are explored. Usually doctrinal issues are also explored at this phase, along with a discussion of how the group's doctrine is twisted and incorporated into the mind control techniques. While arguments about the mind control techniques should be avoided, these are carefully explored with the client—and specific examples are given on how the group practices each technique. Specific known doctrinal aberrations are used to illustrate these various controlling techniques. There are different ways to introduce mind control techniques. Many people have found it fruitful to show a videotape of the ABC Television After School presentation, "The Wave." Based on a true story, "The Wave" shows how a high school teacher models the principles of mind control used in Nazi Germany to take over most of the school in just two weeks. Other videos on other cult issues can be presented as well.

All facts presented about the group *must* be documented. Rumor or hearsay are not employed by professional exit counselors. Confidentiality is respected at all times, and counselors do not pry for details anyone is reluctant to reveal. No professional counselor will reveal the identity or conversations of his or her client to any others without permission from the client.

16. If the cult member personally decides that the group is not right, and they wish to leave, the exit counselor needs to cover important issues relative to helping the person thoroughly understand the experience and speed up the recovery process. The following is a summary of what exit counselor Carol Giambalvo says after a successful intervention:

> Sometimes we hear the phrase "I was deprogrammed" or "I was exit counselled." I'd like to address that for a minute. It's important for you to know that I don't think anyone did anything to you these last few days—except provide you with additional information. When you joined the group, you made the best decision you could have made given the information you received at the time. Your family simply gave you the opportunity to evaluate some new information, and now you've re-evaluated your initial decision based on full and complete information.
>
> So, in the future, if you ever feel embarrassed about being in a cult, remember that you left the group because you made a good decision, based on your personal integrity. Remember this, especially if and when you hear members of your former

group say you left because you are sinning
or because of some other negative thing
about you. That will hurt. But remember,
they have to say those things to justify
their staying a part of it. You just remember *your* reasons for leaving are good
ones.[7]

17. The counselor will strongly advise parents to give the
returning family member room to grow. It is tempting
for parents to hover over their newly returned "lost
sheep," but counselors will try to enable parents to
resist these inclinations.

18. Since not all interventions are successful in helping the
child to leave the group, certain matters should be
covered by the counselor before the intervention ends.

- There should be a review of information about
the group. If the child from the onselt does not
want to hear information about the group, then
attempt to set up a secondary goal of increasing
family communication.

- The counselor should set the stage for further
dialogue now that the family is more open and
has communicated frankly and lovingly about
these issues.

- The client should be prepared for how the group
may treat her when she returns. Tell the client
that the leader may want a thorough debriefing
and may possibly even scold her for not inform-
ing him about the intervention earlier. The client
should be forewarned that the group may try to
distort what really happened during the exit
counseling.[8]

- Possible negative consequences should be mentioned, should the member choose to remain in
the cult. For example, any criminal activity that

has come to light may be presented to the proper legal authorities. Or, the parents may well cut off any financial aid they have been sending. Stick to the consequences, whatever you decide that they must be. Do nothing that will enable the client to have an easier life in the cult because of a decision to stay. Make the cult member come to grips with the results his actions have produced.

Parents will be immensely discouraged and sad if their child decides not to leave the group, but even so, an effective intervention will actually enhance communications and restore bonds with the family. When these bonds are intact and strong, the family member will not feel threatened to talk to parents when they later grow disillusioned with the cult. Any intervention that enhances communication is a success.

14

PITFALLS TO RECOVERY

Making new friends isn't so easy. There's so much lost time and there aren't that many people out there who can understand what you went through. At a party do you say, "I just spent six years with the Unification Church, but I'm into stocks and bonds now"? There is this sense of having a hole in your life and having to explain it. It's important to find a healthy way to do this, because the way you deal with the experience will determine the rest of your life.

—Robert Chin, former member of
the Unification Church

Each person suffering from trauma or injury usually has the capacity to recover. In this chapter I will point out some pitfalls on the road to recovery from the trauma of cultic involvement, and then provide some guidelines for speeding up the recovery process.

I have already listed a number of "myths" surrounding the cultic experience. I want to restate these myths here, because it is very important for recovering cultists to recognize them. If one leaves a cult and surrounds himself or herself with some well-intended people trying to help but believing in one or more of these myths, the recovery process may be delayed or sidetracked.

THE SIX MYTHS ABOUT CULTISM

1. Ex-cult members do not have psychological problems. Their problems are wholly spiritual.
2. Ex-cult members *do* have psychological disorders. But these people come from clearly "non-Christian" cults.
3. Both Christians and non-Christian cultic groups can produce psychological problems, but the people involved must have had prior psychological problems that would have surfaced regardless of what group they joined.
4. While normal non-Christians may get involved with cults, born-again evangelical Christians will not. Even if they did, their involvement would not affect them quite so negatively.
5. Christians can and do get involved in these aberrational groups, and they can get hurt emotionally, but all they really need is some good Bible teaching and a warm, caring Christian fellowship.
6. Perhaps the best way for former cult members to receive help is to seek professional therapy with a psychologist, psychiatrist, or other mental health counselor.

As parents of a son or daughter who has left a cult, it is crucial that you do not subscribe to these myths. If you or anyone connected with your child holds these false beliefs and communicates them, there will be a double sense of victimization. The first sense of victimization is from the cult itself. The young person feels hurt, betrayed, confused, angry, violated, anxious, and perhaps depressed as a result of their cult experience. The second sense of victimization comes when friends, helpers, or family perpetuate the myths about cultism. These myths work themselves out in everyday conversation in such questions and comments as:

- I certainly could think of some others who might join a cult, but you were the *last* person I would have expected.

- Why go to counseling? You know you were deceived in your spiritual walk. What you need to do is repent of your sins so that the deceiver cannot tempt you.

- Why are you complaining so? Your group wasn't a cult—it preached the gospel. Perhaps you're bitter and need to get your heart right with God.

- Perhaps you are not committed enough. Leaving was just an excuse for not totally surrendering your heart to God and for using your rebellion as an excuse to criticize this group. Take the beam out of your own eye first.

- People who join these groups are troubled or have come from dysfunctional homes. I guess I was wrong in assuming you didn't have those problems.

- Why aren't you reading your Bible? After all, the Word is truth and that is what will help heal you. You need to get back into Bible study and serious fellowship; otherwise, the people at church are going to start wondering about you.

- You started slacking off on your Bible study and prayer during college. If you had kept them up, the group involvement wouldn't have deceived you so much and you wouldn't be in the shape you are in now.

When one who has left and is trying to stay away from a cultic group hears these statements, the message that comes through is, "Something is wrong with you." "You must have some psychological problems." "Your spiritual life isn't right." "You are rebellious." If the ex-cultist hears and believes these messages, recovery is all but impossible until the erroneous thinking is corrected. Regardless of one's spiritual or psychological health, whether one is weak or strong, cultic involvement can happen to anyone.

THE STAGES OF RECOVERY

As parents, what is the first thing you should do when your child comes home from a cult? First, take care of any medical or nutritional needs. Make sure that your child is physically healthy. Then, assess which stage of recovery your son or daughter is in. At Wellspring, we see that people usually go through three stages of recovery after leaving a cult.

Stage I Recovery

Exit Counseling and Confronting Denial

If your child continues to be unduly influenced in any way by the cult, consider exit counseling. It takes quite some time for those leaving cults to know what happened to them, and they still operate under shame and guilt over their cultic involvement. One must realize that cults use powerful techniques of manipulation. In reality, your child was victimized by the cult.[1] The major problem for those not undergoing some form of exit counseling is denial. Many continue to believe they were somehow responsible for their fate. It is difficult for them to accept that their lives were not always completely under their own control. Denial shows itself in withdrawal from family and friends, statements that "I'm fine," defensiveness about the group's problem, and refusal to seek help.[2] Such denial must be countered by clearly showing the realities of cult dynamics. Former cult members need to see how they were lured into the movement, what vulnerabilities the cult exploited, and how the principles of mind control were used to keep them in the cult.[3]

Emotional Needs

Cults lure people for many reasons, but perhaps primarily because of the relationships that the experience offers. The involvement is an intensely personal experience. Correspondingly, recovery must be as intense and personal. The therapist, counselor, pastor, and parent must be able to relate to the ex-member's emotional needs for acceptance, belonging, friendship, and love.[4] Harold Busséll notes that while he seldom sees evangelicals enter cultic groups for doctrinal reasons, the main factors that make a group attractive are the cult's emphases on group sharing, community, and caring.[5]

Refuting Error

Other areas should be thoroughly addressed when working with ex-members. First, a sound intellectual and theological refutation of the group's teachings needs to be done, for this is one of the several crucial elements in the former member's recovery. In my years of working with former cultists, I can recall only a few parents who felt qualified to tackle the entire exit counseling process themselves. Most do not feel qualified by virtue of the fact that they lack the doctrinal expertise to refute the cult's teachings. This is why many approach experienced exit counselors.

Another area that needs to be addressed is ethical. How did the cult collect and use money? Did it use methods of thought reform or other deceptive practices?[6] As parents, you can be of great service to exit counselors by providing the information you gleaned in your research on the cult. Exit counselors need much information. Even the best of them will not have all the necessary information on a given group because there are thousands of cults. Parents can be an invaluable resource to counselors.

Recovering Fellowship

In recovering from cultic life, one of the things that takes the longest to resolve is the search for the love, fellowship, and caring that was experienced while in the group. It is extremely important that a trusting relationship be established between the former member and the helper. One study showed that only one-half of exiting cult members who sought help were able to engage in a successful relationship with a counselor.[7] Therefore, the counselor, pastor, and church body must be willing to provide warmth and care to the former member, but they should not try to become a substitute for the intense "social high" experienced by the ex-member in the group. The tremendous fellowship and warmth that the ex-member often longs for is an "artificial high." The group experience felt great, but was it produced by the Holy Spirit? Or was it really more like the feeling of euphoria produced by some drugs?

There are many group processes that can make people feel euphoric. "Moonies" have told me of the tremendous feelings of rapture, love, and warmth that they have experienced at some of their Unification Church services. Members from The Way International also have told me how they sensed the presence of God in their conferences. Ex-members of Great Commission International often long for the type of fellowship they experienced while active in that group. And former members of The Bible Speaks tell how good they felt after attending their services, even calling it a "buzz." A woman I counseled continued actively to attend a charismatic sect even after it had nearly destroyed her family, admitting that the people put her under guilt and that the group estranged her from the family. Why did she go? Because she "felt so good" when she was there. Many former members of cultic groups refer to the experience as a "high" or as "getting high."

A Christian friend returned from a Buddhist meeting and related how she too was moved by the testimonies and the group's singing. She became quite caught up in the meeting, and felt particularly enraptured. This is what happens in the cults and in many churches. Longing for the duplication of these kinds of experiences can be one of the most difficult problems for ex-cultists to overcome. They have learned to love a euphoric feeling, and understandably they begin a search to find that same feeling outside the cult. It becomes in essence an addiction.

These "highs" (which are certainly not unique to Christianity) can be psychologically and spiritually unhealthy.[8] Because the experience produces in the member a strong sense of dependence on the group and its leaders, counselors must be very careful not to foster a similar dependency towards themselves. Dependency conflicts are typically a major problem for ex-members. Good rehabilitation will seek to achieve a movement away from dependency towards group support and healthy relationships.

Recognizing Floating

These "highs" are part of what is known as altered states of consciousness—states between waking and sleeping "that differ from those usually experienced in the world of everyday reality. Included are states such as those induced by creative work, meditation, drugs, sleep, alcohol, and hypnosis."[9] When an ex-cultist returns to the "high" after leaving a cult, it is called "floating." It is also called "floating" when one snaps back into the shame-based motivations experienced while in the cult and believes anew that the cult was right. Floating is handled by discovering what triggers the episodes and then dealing with the triggers.

Types of triggers include:

- *Visual*—certain colors, pictures, hand signals, symbols, smiles
- *Verbal*—songs, jargon, Scripture verses, slogans, types of laughter, mantras, decrees, prayers, tongues speaking, curses
- *Physical*—touches, handshakes, kisses, hugs
- *Smell*—incense, perfume of leader, foods
- *Tastes*—foods[10]

The first step in recovery from floating is to identify these triggers and the loaded language that gives meaning to the visual trigger. For example, the visual trigger may be a book that has been forbidden by the cult. Seeing the book causes thoughts like, "This is the work of the devil." Loaded language is any thought-stopping cliché that is used in manipulative groups to prevent critical thinking. For example, simple tiredness is reinterpreted as "running in the flesh," and is used to discourage people from claiming fatigue or stress. Not wanting to go to every scheduled meeting is labeled "rebellion" and as possessing an "insubmissive spirit." Such loaded language is not easily forgotten even after exiting a cult. It sidetracks critical analysis, disrupts communications, and may produce confusion, anxiety, terror, and guilt.[11]

Undoing the language of the cult requires a hard look at what words and phrases mean. The mind must be taught to rethink the meaning of language. Because cults misuse words and use loaded language, one ex-cultist recommends concentrating on crossword puzzles and other word games as an aid to reground one's conception of the true sense of words.[12] In addition, ex-cultists must learn to challenge the factual claims of loaded language phrases.

Former cult members must be taught to identify such words and phrases that have a special or loaded meaning to them. A cult counselor or other expert can help these people to see the meaning of the verse in its context, if certain Bible passages hold loaded meanings. One simple way for ex-cultists to help themselves is to look words up in a dictionary and then compare those meanings with what the cult taught. The member should be encouraged to spend a good bit of time reading in areas unrelated to the former cult, something else that will help with reprogramming into learning the meaning of words.

Such exercises are crucial for any recovering cultists who feel powerless because they do not know how language was used to control them. Empowerment and control are essential ingredients to recovery from cultic involvement.

Understanding Trauma

In coming to grips with what has happened to the ex-cultist, it is quite helpful to employ the victim or trauma model. According to this model, victimization and the resulting distress it causes are due to the shattering of three basic assumptions that the victim held about the world and the self. These assumptions are the belief in personal invulnerability, the perception of the world as meaningful, and the perception of oneself as positive.[13] The former cult member has been traumatized, deceived, conned, used, and often emotionally and mentally abused while serving the group or the group's leader. Like other victims of such things as criminal acts, war atrocities, rape, and serious illness, ex-cultists often reexperience the painful memories of their group involvement. Trauma also causes many to lose interest in the outside world, feel detached from society, and display limited emotions.[14]

The Nature of Thought Reform

Thought reform techniques can also be viewed as a type of trauma model. Ex-cultists in Stage I of their recovery process must thoroughly understand if and how they were under the influence of a thought reform regimen.

The classic study on thought reform techniques as used by Chinese Communists in the late 1940s and early 1950s was done by Robert J. Lifton.[15] Lifton later found that the same principles of thought reform were also practiced in religious cults.[16] Lifton lists eight definitive criteria for a thought reform program.

1. Milieu Control

This is control of the communication within the group environment that results in a significant degree of isolation from the surrounding society. It includes other techniques aimed at restricting member contact with the outside world and curtailing critical, rational judgments. Some groups utilize milieu control with overwork, busyness, and continual meetings.

The cult builds a wall around the person as shelter from the outside world. The purpose of that wall is to control the amount of information that one receives from the outside. Cults control information through (1) their teachings on doctrinal as well as non-doctrinal matters, (2) their activities, and (3) physically isolating the members from worldly and unspiritual non-members.

Typically cults teach that nearly everything outside the cult is evil, polluted, worldly, and unspiritual. Consequently, even parents are viewed as an unedifying or evil influence. Old friends, familiar activities and innocent interests are viewed with disdain. Hence, to keep oneself pure, the devotee is taught to avoid or severely limit contact with such outside sources. Frequently certain books, magazines, movies or TV shows are outright forbidden. To keep the boundary real, some clear threat to the member is given if they are caught reading forbidden literature.

Another way the cult curtails outside contact is by group activities. Group followers are usually kept extremely busy going to meetings and Bible studies, studying cultic literature, evangelizing, praying, or working for the good of the group. In reality, there is little time for any meaningful interaction with outside resources.

Some cults foster milieu control by physical isolation, requiring adherents to live in communes, to room together, or to reside in some rural training camp. Any contact with the outside is severely limited, and when it does occur it is usually in a group setting and is almost always focused on recruiting new members.

2. Mystical Manipulation

Mystical manipulation is the claim to divine authority or spiritual advancement that allows the leader to reinterpret events as he or she wishes, or make prophecies or pronouncements at will, all for the purpose of controlling group members.

Mystical manipulation also produces the "high" or the "buzz" that enthusiasts feel for their group. Mystical manipulation can occur through charismatic and dynamic speaking, emotional and rousing singing, stirring testimonials, long hours of work with little sleep, poor nutrition, chanting, speaking in tongues, and physical contact such as warm hugging and embracing. These experiences can be combined in a cultic setting to produce a tremendous sense of euphoria that is almost impossible to reproduce outside the group. This euphoria is then labeled "the presence of God," "the moving of the Holy Spirit," "the sign of God's presence," or "inner enlightenment."

3. Demand for Purity

The world is viewed as black and white, right and wrong, good and evil, and group members are constantly exhorted to strive for purity and perfection. To a devoted follower of a cult, one's entire life becomes devoted to becoming a "pure" devotee, pleasing to the leadership, winning approval or at least simply avoiding rejection. To be rejected from the cult is to risk annihilation. The old self must be slowly destroyed; the outside world is now viewed as wicked. One would lose everything to be rejected from the group. Rejection is to face the "dispensing of one's existence." Consequently, cultists try hard to please, to confess, and to become more pure in order to avoid the possible fate of total rejection. Consequently, guilt and shame are common and powerful control devices.

In this way, the full range of responses that we as humans have with one another is emasculated. No longer is there room for playfulness, humor, creativity, questioning, doubt, fear, anxiety, or longing. Abusive and authoritarian groups often view such emotions as sinful and a part of the lower self. The result? Cultists live a life that isn't their own. It is the life of unwitting hypocrisy and the plastered-on smile, a life that has become so constricted that neither the Holy Spirit nor the human spirit can prevail.

4. The Cult of Confession

Serious (and often not so serious) sins, as defined by the group, are to be confessed, either privately to a personal monitor or publicly to the group at large. The confession practice is clearly much more extreme than the normal confessional practices of the church.

5. *The "Sacred Science"*

This is the belief that the doctrine of the group is ultimate Truth, beyond all questioning or disputing. The leader of the group is also above criticism as the final spokesperson for God on earth.

The "sacred science" of the cult consists of the various doctrines and teachings of the group. The teachings are sacred because of the belief that they are infallible or have originated from an indisputable source, divine revelation, or inspiration—thus, they are beyond questioning. The "science" aspect of the sacred science means that the teachings are precise and able to explain everything. In other words, the system that practices sacred science claims to have an answer for nearly everything—from health to economics, world affairs, psychology, and spirituality. One cultic Bible school uses a single textbook for their psychology classes— the Bible. Typically, many cults think the Bible says everything there is to say on any and all topics, especially psychology and even matters of physical and mental health.

In a sacred science there is no truth outside their own "science" or exclusive view of the truth. The cult believes that it has the corner on the truth. No other group does. In contrast, the truth held by other established religions is open to question, argument, and examination. In aberrational Christian churches, the sacred science may concede some truth outside the camp, but would hold that no other churches have the full blessing, commitment, vision, or dedication that it has. Only their group possesses the sacred science. Thus, this truth must be shared with others. The entire earth becomes the target for new recruits.

6. Loading the Language

The group develops a unique jargon, often indecipherable to outsiders. This jargon consists of numerous loaded words and phases which the members understand (or think they do), but which act as "thought-terminating clichés." For example, any facts that threaten the group's integrity may be called, "lies of the devil."

7. Doctrine Over Person

Personal experiences of individual group members are subordinated to the "Truth" that is held in common by the group. Contrary experiences of what is or is not true must be denied or reinterpreted to fit the accepted doctrine of the group. The collected doctrine is always more important than individual beliefs and personalities. Group thought takes precedence over individual thought, one's personality, interests, health—virtually everything.

For example, some cults teach that being an artist, musician, or physician is settling for God's "second best." These and other pursuits are a waste of time because so many people could be won to the cause during the time one would have to take to pursue a career in the arts or science. Those not naturally gifted or inclined to lead are made to feel unspiritual and immature for not being aggressive and taking leadership. Certain thoughts are now viewed as sinful, rebellious, or unspiritual. To question leadership is a certain sign of rebellion. The self is remolded and the pre-cult personality is viewed as sinful.

During recovery the entire doctrine-over-person process must be carefully sorted out. The pre-cult personality must be seen as part of the self. Certain careers, thoughts, or questions are to be seen as healthy and not sinful. Careful questioning of the recovering cultist will help reveal how much of the pre-cult personality was restrained and how the process of questioning itself was curtailed during life in the suppressive group.

8. Dispensing of Existence

The group claims to itself the prerogative to decide who has the right to exist and who does not. Of course, this is usually held non-literally, in that it means that those outside the group are considered unspiritual, worldly, satanic, "unconscious," or that they must be converted to the ideas of the group or risk being lost forever. Should they refuse to join the group, they must be rejected as non-existent by the group, and this is so even if they are family members. In rare cases, however, this concept is taken quite literally, as when cults feel they have the right to terminate the outsider's life.

Only when formerly active cultists realize how the self and their boundaries were altered, and how personal feelings were constricted, will the pre-cult personality reemerge. This is the way to recovery. Two very powerful feelings will emerge at this stage: joy over being free and the rage over being violated. Without seeing how thought reform actually works, the former member will be unable to deal with the guilt, fear, shame, and anxiety in anything but a superficial way. Without a real understanding of mind control, whatever one does to come to terms with these feelings will be denied in time.

For one who has been controlled by a cult, the joy of being free, and the rage at understanding what has happened, serve as strong cleansers to the human spirit. These feelings must run their course. It is at this point that healing moves quickly. The person is at Stage II recovery.

Stage II Recovery

Permission to Grieve and Regaining Purpose

At Stage II your son or daughter will be dealing with many disturbing thoughts and questions, including these:

- I feel sad that my friends are still in the group.
- How can I make new friends?
- I can't believe this happened to me.
- I've lost so much time.
- Can I find any legitimate spirituality outside of the cult?
- What can I believe about God?
- How could I have been so stupid?

Stage II is the beginning of the grieving process. At this stage, recovery should focus on helping these people express their grief and regain beliefs about the real world and their true selves. The ex-member must begin again to believe in a meaningful universe and to see themselves as a positive aspect of God's creation.

The cultic experience is often a crisis of faith. At the bottom of many ex-members' beliefs is the question, "How could God allow this to happen to me?" Many feel like fools, while their belief in a "just world" is shattered. They can no longer believe "It won't happen to me." Therefore, a quest for meaning among ex-cultists is paramount. The former member must be helped to regain a belief in his or her individual worth, and in a world that allows room for bad things happening to good people. The ex-member may also need to talk out and relive the trauma again and again, as do the victims of other types of crises.[17] Sadly, the needed and healthy process of talking about the trauma is sometimes short-circuited by well-intended helpers who view such rumination as damaging.

Effective therapy has to be very supportive and

reaffirming, as self-esteem needs to be rekindled. Those who have left cults need to be free of the view that they were solely responsible for their plight. They must be able to forgive themselves. Meaning and trust can be regained, and theological reconstruction can be achieved, when one sees the cult event in view of a benevolent God who truly loves them.[18]

The Need for Reconciliation

Many former cult members realize that their cultic activities unintentionally or even intentionally offended others. It is very healing to go back to those offended and ask for reconciliation. And where this is possible it should be encouraged. While one's *intentions* were not meant to be harmful, recovering cultists realize their *acts* may have been.

Requesting Information

Almost invariably most former members going through Stage II recovery have a lot of questions to ask about the specifics of their group, the Bible (if it was a Bible-based cult), and religion more generally. These questions need to be thoroughly answered. Yet, pastors should beware of the pitfalls in working with former cult members.

The Pastor's Role

Pastors working with recovering cultists should know that their chances for full recovery may depend to a good extent on how similar the church and the pastor are to the extremist group. In other words, if there is a marked similarity between the former group and the present church, then there will be a greater probability that the current church setting will trigger traumatic memories. Consequently, pastors should strongly suggest that ex-members seriously consider buying a new Bible translation, finding a pastor unlike the past leader in personality or teaching style, and attending a church or fellowship providing a welcome contrast to the cultic milieu. Far too often ex-cult members drop out of good churches because they remind them too much of their previous group. It is tragic that they are often viewed more as "backsliders" than victims.

The Need for Support

Professional residential counseling or activity in a support group can certainly help by giving the former cult members strategies to enable them to avoid future victimization by manipulative people. One way to allow former members to regain some sense of their own strength and self-esteem is to find and talk with other former cult members, preferably from the same cultic group. This can offer an important step to recovery. Through this process former members often become close friends. It is very similar to the "war buddies" programs, or the plethora of support groups that have arisen in recent years to help victims of drug or alcohol abuse, divorce, or cancer.

Rediscovering the Gospel

For those leaving aberrational Christian groups, it is essential for them to rediscover the Gospel. In my experience, all aberrational Christian cults distort certain aspects of the Gospel. These are groups that claim to recognize, articulate, and demonstrate the Gospel of Jesus Christ, but nevertheless in one aspect or more do not adhere to the major creeds of the Church nor accept the authority of the Bible as taught by orthodox Christian faith.

Recently I heard of two young women with backgrounds in different cults. The leader of one group justified having sex with some of the women in the church because "God's grace is so great that he can forgive anything." Under the banner of grace, he had oral sex, group masturbation, group sex, and individual sessions of intercourse with the women because "God's grace was so great."

The other woman's sect taught a version of the Gospel that emphasized "mortification of the flesh." For them the essence of the Gospel was to imitate how Jesus "mortified his flesh." Each Christian was to do the same in order to be saved.

Much confusion is caused by cults because their public façade and their public statements of faith seem quite sound. The average person would assume that if a church or association *seems* to be Christian or *claims* to be Christian, that they probably are Christian. But much of the distortion often happens with the communication that goes on within the inner circle of the cult. Here the leader reveals his or her own insights and practices that can be justified because the world is not ready to grasp them. Because of their own claimed spiritual advancement, they can understand and practice these hidden or secret truths that remain unrevealed to all others. And the leader's lucky followers can become a part of this inner circle of more enlightened and more spiritual disciples.

The large body of orthodox Christianity would recognize the extremes of both groups mentioned above as well beyond the bounds of orthodoxy. Many other examples could be given, as in the "Shepherding" movement. One might be hard pressed to find fault with their doctrinal beliefs. As many Christians have discovered, however, their error is in an authority structure that stresses unquestioning submission to leadership in virtually every area of life. This extreme form of authority in the church goes way outside the boundaries of accepted biblical authority.

To many it is frightening that many of these cultic

groups could, with a clear conscience, subscribe to a most orthodox, fundamental, and evangelical statement of faith. But actually they represent a deadly religion of works righteousness. For this reason it is very liberating for former members of such groups or churches to study Paul's letter to the Galatians, and to contrast Paul's message of justification by faith with their group's practices. The Gospel restores meaning to life, and self-esteem is regained. A clear understanding of the Gospel is the single most important issue in a cultist's spiritual recovery and future immunity to further cultic involvement.[19]

Rescuing Others

During Stage II recovery ex-members will often direct some energy into trying to rescue their friends from the cult. Without careful planning such efforts usually prove fruitless. It is always best for ex-members to grow strong themselves before developing plans to help friends. This usually means contacting the friend's parents, family, or close friends, and sharing the information about the group. Once this is done, it is then their decision to plan some method to extricate their family member from the cult. An ill-planned phone call, letter, or article sent directly to the friend still in the cult will usually result in that information getting into the hands of the leader. Invariably, the leader will quickly refute the material and warn against misguided former members attempting to deceive.

Contact by the Cult

Some former cultists don't know what to do if they are contacted by people still in the cult. One must be prepared. Most cults will continue trying to exercise control over former members. Their purpose is first to try to woo the lost sheep back. If they don't succeed, they will attempt "damage control"—that is, they will try to discredit the deserter and limit any contact they may have with those still safely tucked in the cult.

Generally it is fruitless for ex-members to argue with cultists who contact them. The purpose in the contact might be to say "we miss you," "we love you," "we have been so worried about you," "we have been praying for you," or, "we would like to get back with you." It is best for former members to express appreciation for the concern and suggest that perhaps in the future a meeting may be arranged. But don't make any promises. Let them play their cards. If other group members who make contact have sincere questions about their own involvement in the group, then there is the possibility of sharing some information. Otherwise, remarks should be limited.

Threats from the Cult

A more serious concern is actual fear of harm from the cult. Many groups are known to be violent towards ex-members, and protection is very important. The following suggestions come from an experienced exit counselor.[20] The question of protecting ex-cultists is a complex one, and the following checklist includes three stages addressed directly to the ex-cultist:

Stage One: Reality Testing

1. Has your group ever hurt, sued, libeled, slandered, or actually killed or kidnapped someone?
2. Have you ever met anyone who was so harmed?
3. Has anyone in your group admitted to hurting or harassing others?
4. How important were you to the group? Do they have any reason to fear you now that you are out?

5. How emotionally stable is the leader and the group's members?

   Eighty percent of exit-counseling cases do not produce safety concerns. The remaining twenty percent can involve aggressive efforts to contact the person, harassment, and legal threats. This has been called a "hollow threat," and it usually reflects a leader's need to impress the followers.

Stage Two: Putting the Cult on Notice

If you are harassed:
1. Write your cult leader and state emphatically that you are leaving the group and do not wish to be contacted. Send it by registered mail and keep the receipt.
2. Hang up on all cult calls—get an unlisted number if you get crank calls.
3. Go to the police and make a complaint—you may be able to get a restraining order if you are being seriously harassed.
4. Legal harassment from the cult requires you to get professional legal help for yourself.

   The next category involves specific though relatively rare acts or threats against individuals.

Stage Three: Protecting Yourself

If there are direct threats of physical violence:

1. Assess the extent of the threat.
2. Notify law enforcement.
3. Arrange for their help.
4. Take protective countermeasures.
5. Be aware of surveillance.
6. Never travel alone.
7. Monitor telephone calls.

 8. Keep cars protected.
 9. Carefully monitor your family.
10. Alter familiar daily patterns.
11. Keep exterior house lights on at night.
12. Install a home security system.
13. Buy a big or loud dog.
14. Move to another locale.

Reemergence of the Past

Invariably, as Stage II recovery issues are resolving, past issues that are unresolved may surface. These may include:

- Unresolved grief over divorce of parents
- Death of parents or other family members
- Drug/alcohol or other addictions in the family
- Personal problems
- Loneliness
- Unsatisfactory past family relationships
- Unsatisfactory relationships with the opposite sex

A time of crisis may trigger a completely new awareness of unresolved issues. Recently I counseled a young man named Charles, who was raised in a dysfunctional home. As a child, his father left the family and was gone for several years. During this time Charles' mother leaned on him for emotional support. As a result, Charles felt like a smothered and helpless little child. He wanted to be strong and responsible. Bitterness and resentment ensued. To leave this situation, Charles unknowingly joined and then eventually left a cult, working through the various recovery stages.

The cult crisis caused all family members to see their own unresolved problems. They found some books about codependency and discovered that the family had been seriously dysfunctional. Although there was much grief and tears, the denial and resistance were gone. The steps for recovery proceeded rapidly with good progress.

The actual crisis of the reemergence of the past can be an excellent opportunity to improve family relations, heal wounds, and develop patterns of healthy relations that will benefit the next generations.

Stage III Recovery

When you hear your son or daughter or other loved one talk less and less about the cult, and spend more time in career pursuits, relationships, and personal issues, you will know they are in the third stage of recovery. Typically cult experiences prove to be temporary diversions to adulthood. The cult will often seek to thwart or confuse members about career and school aspirations. Often, when students are brought into cultic organizations, cult leaders will have them switch majors or even drop out of school. They might be told that in following the leader's advice they will be more productive for the kingdom, or that God would be more pleased if they changed career direction, or that they would be more effective in getting the gospel out. When the former cult member sees through these diversions, full recovery to spiritual adulthood is highly possible.

Positives of the Cult Experience

As strange as it may sound, there are often some positive benefits to the cultic experience. Perhaps unhealthy shyness has been overcome because the young person has been challenged to accept leadership opportunities. Perhaps an ability to organize and administrate has been learned. After all, anyone in a cult learns about discipline, hard work, long hours, specific job skills, and teamwork. These skills and abilities, when moderated in the confines of true freedom, can serve a person very well indeed. The cult can at least be appreciated for experiences like these.

Recovery of the Whole Self

It is important to extract whatever was positive from the cult experience, and then to relate it to pre-cult aspirations. In my experience, I have found some very insightful clues into a client's personality and interests by exploring with them their childhood activities, dreams, wishes, and talents. Whatever good that comes out of an active cult affiliation can be reapplied toward fulfilling those talents and interests that one had before the cult involvement.

For example, my own childhood was filled with love for the outdoors, nature, fishing, hunting, travel, adventure, and a clear penchant for the informal. When I spent seven years in the city as part of the Great Commission International, my whole personality was put into question. My love for nature and the rural settings didn't seem to fit our group's call to reach the whole world. I began to think more and more that I was somehow less spiritual than others. My love for the arts and for the creative spirit in others didn't seem to fit in the group, either. Life in this fringe group was primarily a passion for duty to reach the world for Christ. Life for me in this context went from "color" to "black and white." Without question, parts of me died during those years in this group. I have been able to take the discipline that I learned in the group into my current career. But I constantly try to recover the parts of me that died during that involvement.

The Self and Christian Commitment

Cults often defend their "black and white" order by pointing to Christ's commands to "deny self" and to "forsake all." Does God really desire a reduced version of ourselves? Why would we have been created in our richness of talent, interests, and temperaments if those things are evil? Aren't we to give the entire self with all its richness to God to be used for his glory and his kingdom?

Christ's call to forsake all, to deny self, to take up our cross, and to have a righteousness greater than the scribes and Pharisees points out the utter impossibility of anyone ever achieving such a state of perfect goodness. We are meant to ask, as Peter asked Jesus when the rich young ruler went away, "Who then can be saved?" Jesus replied that "With man it is impossible, but with God all things are possible."

The Christian life is distorted if we do not keep in mind that it is impossible to be reconciled to God without his free gift of grace through the death of Jesus Christ. It is also distorted when we do not have an affirming acceptance of ourselves. As Christians we do not lose our interests, talents, and personalities when we become believers. What we should lose is our ignorance about God. Human evil is not located in our talents or our personality type, but in the bondage of our very wills. The very act of being reconciled to God provides a way to see growth and healing in our lives, not the denial of them. The act of grace provides the dual miracles of love for God and love for self. Clarifying what the "self" is clarifies that God indeed accepts and affirms who we are.

Sexuality and Dating

Sexuality and dating can be a troublesome problem for those recovering from the cults that distort male and female relationships.

Examples of distorted sexuality abound in cultic groups. Marriages in the Unification Church, for example, are quite often arranged by the Reverend Moon—and often the marriage partners do not speak each other's languages and may not even meet until shortly before the ceremony. University Bible Fellowship, with headquarters in Chicago, has been known to arrange marriages as well.

Many cults do not permit dating at all. Celibacy is quite common among Hare Krishnas, Transcendental Meditation devotees, and members of Ananda Marga Yoga. Still other groups permit dating within the group, but only when chaperoned or approved by the leadership. In the Boston Church of Christ, dating is almost exclusively in the form of double-dating. Recently, some former members of that church told me that there has been some relaxation about this rule. Former members of Great Commission International have told me that dating was forbidden or discouraged. The founder of GCI, Jim McCotter, once wrote that dating is a type of "faction" not unlike other factions that can divide a church.[21] Reports from Maranatha Ministries revealed that dating rules were so strict that one needed permission from the leadership to date, and then one could date only people within the movement. Dating as a single couple was permitted only if engaged.

Many cults teach that all sexual feelings are sinful and lustful. One prime example of this would be the Unification Church, or the "Moonies." Also, the Hare Krishnas take the extreme view that sex is for procreation only, not for pleasure between marriage partners, and may be engaged in only once per month.

By stark contrast, nudity and pre-marital sex is permitted, encouraged, or even required in other cultic groups and churches. One woman reported that members of her church were told to remove their clothes to prove they were "open" to one another. In a Racine, Wisconsin group, leader Larry Yarber "would ask women to open their blouses and bare their breasts to him."[22] Yarber told one woman, "Unzip your pants. You shouldn't be inhibited. God wants your needs to be fulfilled. You don't have a husband right now; you'll have one someday."[23] Other female members reported that Yarber told them the same thing.[24] The women interviewed said that Yarber used sex under the pretext of helping them with their "sexual problems."[25]

John Gottuso, pastor of Park View Christian Fellowship in California, convinced a number of women to become sexually involved with him as an aid to their spiritual life.[26] Another member of Gottuso's church said, "The theme was masturbating your deepest darkest secrets . . . a lot of times he'd challenge men or women to take off their clothes or pants—to demonstrate their genital area or breasts."[27] Other examples from many different groups could be cited. These illustrations are offered as examples of the types of sexuality exhibited in cults—most of which (including Gottuso's) boast evangelical statements of faith.

The broad range of sexual attitudes and practices seen in cults underscores the confusion that arises for many ex-members as they readjust to sexual behavior and values outside the cult.

It is the goal of rehabilitation to allow the former members to see how the group's standards deviated from the accepted norms of dating in our society, from his or her own conscience, and from the Christian heritage. It is not uncommon for former cult members to go to extremes upon leaving a group. The sexually "pure" may become promiscuous, and the sexually active may become rather prudish. Such behavior exposes the damage and abuse of the cult, and the rage of the recovering cult member. Often this rage can be dealt with effectively only through professional counseling.

Longing for Friends in the Cult

Even during Stage III recovery your child will still continue to miss friends left in the cult, and may even desire to get them out. Reasonable approaches to helping a friend can be encouraged, but only when your son or daughter has sufficiently recovered. When former cult members continue to obsess about getting people out, when they are constantly thinking and talking about their friends left in the cult and their desire to assist them, it is wise to explore possible reasons for such strong concerns. Many codependent relationships develop while in the cult, and these can certainly continue when one leaves. Excessive guilt over recruiting some of these people gives some members an inordinate desire to rescue friends.

CONCLUSION

These are the issues and the steps to recovery that one will experience when leaving a cult. It is unfair and unrealistic to suggest that parents are to guide or counsel their loved one through the recovery process on their own. The best method is a few weeks of an intensive, professional rehabilitation program, such as the Wellspring program. But the process is not easy. Many get stuck on the road to recovery. Some avoid church altogether, or may "church hop" forever. Some have trouble in their professional or personal lives. Recovering cultists who continue to experience difficulties should be professionally evaluated by an expert in cults to determine the need for rehabilitative programs.

The Parents' Role

Parents should try not to control their child's future. Bill and Lorna Goldberg have worked with former cultists and their families for over fifteen years. They have consistently observed that parents naturally regress during a time of crisis—and a child in a cult or recovering from one is surely in a crisis! During regression, parents will do what they did when their child was much younger—direct and control. However, only your children can tell you what they need. Listen to them to know how to help. You can do no better than to offer love, understanding, and support.

There are some specific guidelines you can follow when your child first returns home from a cult. First, you should curtail nearly all activities that were specific to the group. This may include avoiding certain songs or reading certain religious materials. It may even include avoiding certain exercise regimens. For some recovering cultists, religious activities are best picked up slowly with a nice break in the interim. Besides these guidelines, let your son or daughter tell you their needs. They may want to talk to other ex-members, or request counseling, or do additional study and research on the cult problem on their own. Support them in these decisions.[28]

At base, parents want to know if their kids will be okay. This is the most common question parents ask when their child returns home from a cult. I have tried in the last chapters of this book to help you know the three different stages of recovery, and to determine where your child is in the stages. The book provides resources for you and your family member who is exiting a cultic environment. But life offers no guarantees, and that applies to the success of post-cult recovery as well. The chances of becoming whole after exiting a cultic situation increase if each issue is clearly addressed, and if your kids sense your genuine warmth, love, care, and understanding. This recovery time can become a tremendous opportunity for the entire family to reflect, grow, and chart new directions in life with a fuller and healthier viewpoint.

The Recovery of Faith

I wish the cult-recovery experience on no one. For me and for so many others, that experience shook the foundations of our faith to the roots and left us feeling helpless and in despair. But it also enabled us in time to see as never before the power of God's love, grace, and mercy.

Tragically, some people never seem to recover fully from the experience, and the continued unresolved spiritual issues are an anguishing reality for many former members. As their parents and friends, we are struck by their great pain. We can do no more than to forebear and travail with them through their time of suffering. There are no simple answers, but genuine love never fails.

———————————

For more information on post-cult rehabilitative counseling in a residential facility, contact Dr. Paul Martin at:

Wellspring Retreat and Resource Center
P.O. Box 67
Albany, OH 45710
614-698-6277

NOTES

PREFACE

1. Joan Ross and Michael Langone, *Cults: What Parents Should Know* (New York: Lyle Stuart, 1989), 20.
2. Robert R. Hinnells, ed., *The Dictionary of Religion* (New York: Viking Penguin, Inc., 1984), 119–20.
3. Robert Dugan, Jr., *Winning the New Civil War* (Portland, Ore.: Multnomah Press, 1991), 171.
4. Ibid., 169.
5. I don't at all mean to imply that it is less tragic when people of lower intellectual ability or social status join cults. It simply has been my experience that the cults do not normally target the average or below-average student, and they are not too successful when they do try. I do not know why; I simply don't see them coming to Wellspring for help with any degree of consistency.

INTRODUCTION

1. Steve Hassan, *Combatting Cult Mind Control* (Rochester, Vermont: Park Street Press, 1990).

CHAPTER 1: WHAT IS A CULT?

1. Harold Busséll, *Unholy Devotion* (Grand Rapids, Mich.: Zondervan Publishing House, 1983), 12.
2. Walter Martin, *The New Cults* (Ventura, Calif.: Vision House, 1980), 16.
3. Ronald Enroth, *What is a Cult?* (Downers Grove, Ill.: InterVarsity Press, 1982), 12.
4. Paul R. Martin, "Dispelling the Myths," *Christian Research Journal* (Winter/Spring, 1989): 9–14.

5. Enroth, *What Is a Cult?*, 16.
6. personal telephone conversation with Rev. Wm. Kent Burtner, consultant on cults and thought reform programs.
7. Ross and Langone, *Cults: What Parents Should Know* (New York: Carol Publishing Group, 1988), 20.
8. From *Cults: A Conference for Scholars and Policy Makers*, sponsored by the American Family Foundation, the UCLA Neuropsychiatric Institute and the Johnson Foundation, September 1985.
9. From Enroth, *The Lure of the Cults*, 22–25. [Note: New "religious movements" is a non-pejorative term used to describe "a wide variety of organizations having some type of spiritual orientation that is unconventional. Generally, the term refers to groups arising out of the sixties spiritual ferment." So defined in Diane Choquette, compiler, *New Religious Movements in the United States and Canada* (Westport, Conn.: Greenwood Press, 1985), viii, 3.] The author added the extremist political/social movements category.
10. See Jamie Buckingham, "The End of the Discipleship Era," *Ministry Today* (January/February 1990); and the Assemblies of God General Presbytery, *The Discipling and Submission Movement* (Springfield, Mo.: Assemblies of God Publishing House, 1976).
11. These figures come from the American Family Foundation, the Cult Awareness Network, and the Christian Research Institute.

CHAPTER 2: FRINGE CHURCHES

1. Ronald Enroth, *Youth, Brainwashing and the Extremist Cults* (Grand Rapids, Mich.: Zondervan Publishing House, 1977); *What is a Cult?* (Downers Grove, Ill.: InterVarsity Press, 1982); *The Lure of the Cults* (Downers Grove, Ill.: Intervarsity Press, 1987).
2. Ronald Enroth, "Voices from the Fringe," *Moody Monthly* (October 1989): 94–104; "Churches on the Fringe," *Eternity* (October 1986): 17–22; *Churches That Abuse* (Grand Rapids, Mich.: Zondervan Publishing House, 1992).

CHAPTER 3: WHY DO PEOPLE JOIN CULTS?

1. Neil Maron and Joel Braverman, "Family Environment as a Factor in Vulnerability to Cult Involvement," *Cultic Studies Journal* 1 (1988): 31.
2. Harold Busséll, *Unholy Devotion* (Grand Rapids, Mich.: Zondervan Publishing House, 1983); "Why Evangelicals Are Attracted to the Cults," *Moody Monthly* (March 1985): 111–13.
3. Una McManus and John Copper, *Dealing With Destructive Cults* (Grand Rapids, Mich.: Zondervan Publishing House, 1984), 13–25.

CHAPTER 4: MYTHS OF CULT INVOLVEMENT

1. Margaret Singer, "Coming Out of the Cults," *Psychology Today* (January 1979): 72–82. The following section on the "myths" originally appeared in Paul R. Martin, "Dispelling the Myths" in the *Christian Research Journal* (Spring 1989). The *Christian Research Journal* is published by the Christian Research Institute, Box 500, San Juan Capistrano, CA 92693 (714) 855-9926. Used by permission.
2. Sects that are doctrinally evangelical believe in the full authority of the Bible, salvation by grace alone through trusting in the death of Jesus Christ, the personal return of Jesus Christ at the end of history, and the eternal reward for the saved and eternal punishment for those who reject the message of salvation.
3. Francis A. Schaeffer, *True Spirituality* (Wheaton, Ill.: Tyndale House Publishers, 1971), 132–33. (See all of Chapter 10, "Substantial Healing of Psychological Problems," 123–33.)
4. Saul V. Levine, "Radical Departures," *Psychology Today*, August 1984, 27; Singer, 1979; Neil Maron, "Family Environment as a Factor in Vulnerability to Cult Involvement," *Cultic Studies Journal* 5, no. 1 (1988): 23–43; John G. Clark, M.D., "Cults," *Journal of the American Medical Association*, 242, no. 3, pp. 279–80; Lorna Goldberg and William Goldberg, "Group Work with Former Cultists," *Social Work* 27, no. 2 (March 1982): 165–70.

5. By this I refer to groups that adhere to the major historical creeds of the Church.

6. These are groups that do *not* use the Bible as their primary source of divine authority. Instead, these groups may use other sacred texts, such as the Muslim *Koran*, the Hindu *Bhagavad Gita*, or a text written by a contemporary cult leader, such as the Reverend Moon's *Divine Principle*.

7. Flavil R. Yeakley, Jr., *The Discipling Dilemma* (Nashville, Tenn.: The Gospel Advocate Co., 1988), 23–28.

8. Generally "dominion theology" and "kingdom theology" in this context refers to the teaching that Christians have the spiritual right and authority to rule the world. Such groups feel compelled to see Christians take over the government, the schools, businesses. Essentially, they want to take dominion over the earth. However, despite the breadth of their agenda, there is no evidence that these groups are planning any forceful or militaristic approaches to reach their goals. They generally want to work through the democratic process to achieve these.

9. See "The Week the Walls Came Down," by Lee Grady, *Ministries Today* (May/June 1990): 84ff.

10. Of the clients who have been treated at Wellspring Retreat and Resource Center, the levels of psychological distress as measured by the Millon Multiaxial Inventory (MCMI) did not appreciably differ (as measured by multivariate analysis of covariance) regardless of the cult type. In other words, those coming from "fringe" Christian groups demonstrated MCMI scores that were equal to or higher than scores of those from other cultic groups. The method of leaving the cult (whether through deprogramming, voluntary counseling, or just walking out on one's own) did not significantly affect the initial MCMI test profile prior to entering the Wellspring rehabilitation program.

11. See note 4.

12. See note 4.

13. Augustine of Hippo, *Sermons on the Old Testament*, Number 46, "On Pastors," excerpt entitled "Shepherds

Who Kill Their Sheep," reprinted in *Pastoral Renewal* 13, no. 4 (January/February 1989): 23–24.

14. This story is from Paul Martin, "Dispelling the Myths," 9–10.

15. Bussél, *Unholy Devotion*, 9–10; J. L. Williams, *Identifying and Dealing with the Cults* (Burlington, NC: New Directions Evangelistic Ministries, 1975), 2.

16. Flo Conway and Jim Siegelman, "Information Disease: Have Cults Created a New Mental Illness?" *Science Digest* (January 1982): 86–92; and Flo Conway, James H. Siegelman, Carl W. Carmichael, and John Coggins, "Information Disease: Effects of Covert Induction and Deprogramming," *Update* 10, no. 2 (June 1986): 45–47, and *Update* 10, no. 3 (September 1986): 63–65.

17. See Jerry Paul MacDonald, "Reject the Wicked Man— Coercive Persuasion and Deviance Production: A Study of Conflict Management," *Cultic Studies Journal* 5 (1988): 59–121.

18. Levine, "Radical Departures," 27, though Levine at times suggests that cultic experiences are benign.

19. Christina Maslach, "Burnout: A Social Psychological Analysis," in *The Burnout Syndrome*, edited by John W. Johnes (Park Ridge, Ill.: London House Press, 1981), 42–43.

20. Nathaniel Brandon, *Honoring the Self* (New York: Bantam Books, 1983), 221.

21. Brandon, *The Psychology of Self-Esteem* (New York: Bantam Books, 1969), 245.

22. Albert Ellis, *Reason and Emotion in Psychotherapy* (Secaucus, N.J.: Lyle Stuart, 1962), 146.

CHAPTER 5: SPOTTING A CULT

1. Everett L. Shostrom and Dan Montgomery, *The Manipulators* (Nashville, Tenn.: Abingdon Press, 1990), 29.

2. Ibid., 27.

3. Ibid., 27, 28.

4. Ibid., 28.

5. Ibid.

6. Ibid., 29–30.

7. Ibid., 82.

8. Ibid., 84.

9. Ibid., 89.

10. Harold Busséll, *Unholy Devotion* (Grand Rapids, Mich.: Zondervan Publishing House), 62, 63.

11. E.g., Richard V. Pierard, "Schaeffer on History," in *Reflections on Francis Schaeffer*, Ronald Ruegsegger, ed. (Grand Rapids, Mich.: Zondervan Publishing House), 209; Rousas J. Rushdoony, *This Independent Republic* (Fairfax, Va.: Thoburn Press, 1978), 24, 25; Junius Brutus, *A Defense of Liberty Against Tyrants* (Edmonton, Alberta, Canada: Still Waters Revival Books, 1989), 31.

12. Westminster Confession, chapter 20, paragraph 2, "Of Christian Liberty and Liberty of Conscience."

13. Cited in Sandy Andron, *Cultivating Cult Evading* (Miami: Central Agency for Jewish Education, 1983), Appendix F.

CHAPTER 6: THE HEALTHY FAMILY

1. Mark I. Sirkin and Bruce A. Grellong, "Cult vs. Noncult—Jewish Families: Factors Influencing Conversion," *Cultic Studies Journal* 5, no. 1 (1988): 2; Lita Linzer Schwartz and Florence W. Kaslow, "The Cult Phenomenon Historical, Sociological, and Familial Factors Contributing to their Development and Appeal," *Marriage and Family Review* 4, nos. 3 & 4 (Fall/Winter 1981): 3–15.

2. Neil Maron and Joel Braverman, "Family Environment as a Factor in Vulnerability to Cult Involvement," *Cultic Studies Journal* 1 (1988): 23.

3. Sirkin and Grellong, 2.

4. Ibid., 2, 18.

5. *Maron and Braverman*, 31.

6. Donald L. Sloat, *The Dangers of Growing Up in a Christian Home* (Nashville, Tenn.: Thomas Nelson, 1986); *Growing Up Holy and Wholly* (Brentwood, Tenn.: Wolgemuth and Hyatt Publishers, 1990).

7. Sloat, *Growing Up Holy and Wholly*, 105–64. Used by permission.

8. Ibid., 39–40. Used by permission.

9. Edith Schaeffer, *What is a Family?* (Old Tappan, N.J.: Fleming H. Revell, 1975), 37.

CHAPTER 7: PARENTING TIPS

1. Toxic parents are those who inflict ongoing trauma, abuse, and denigration on their children, and in most cases continue to do so even after their children are grown.
2. Philip A. Captain, *Eight Stages of Christian Growth* (Englewood Cliffs, N.J.: Prentice Hall Inc., 1984), 66.
3. Alan and Beth Niquette, *Building Your Christian Defense System* (Minneapolis, Minn.: Bethany House Publishers), 1988.
4. Clyde Narramore, "Abuse from 'Good' Parents," *Discovery Digest* 13, no. 4 (1988): 10–13.
5. James M. Harper and Margaret H. Hoopes, *Uncovering Shame* (New York: W.W. Norton and Co., 1990), 90.
6. James Dobson, *The Strong Willed Child* (Wheaton, Ill.: Tyndale House Publishers, 1978).
7. Dr. Ken Magid and Carole A. McKelvey, *High Risk: Children Without a Conscience* (New York: Bantam Books, 1987), 1–26.

CHAPTER 8: CULT-PROOFING YOUR SCHOOLS

1. See letter from James C. Dobson (dated October 27, 1971) to Mr. Rich Little of Quest Inc., 270 N. Main St., Findley, Ohio 45840.
2. Letter from Mrs. Barbara Hanna to James C. Dobson, dated January 10, 1981.
3. Ibid.
4. Letter to Professor and Mrs. Robert Crowner (board member of *Quest*) from Jason Adelson, Professor of Psychology at University of Michigan, dated January 29, 1986.
5. Ibid.
6. See letter dated May 6, 1985 from Mrs. Barbara Hanna to Betty Lewis. Copies of all the above letters may be obtained from the Child Care Community Organization, Box 278, Eudora, Kans. 66025. Also obtainable through this address is *The Old Paths vs. the New Age* (1985).
7. "U.S. Commission of Education Task Force on Global Education Report," *Developing Global Education Teaching States* (1979): 3. Distributed by the office for

Equity Education, the office of the superintendent of Public Instruction, Old Capitol Building, Olympia, WA 98504.

8. Eric Buehrer, *The New Age Masquerade* (Brentwood, Tenn.: Wolgemuth and Hyatt, 1990), 16–20.

9. Ibid., 29.

10. Ibid., 56.

11. Ibid., 70–80.

12. Eileen Lunch, et. al., *Evaluation Report of the Robert Mueller School for the Southern Association of Colleges and Schools* (October 1984), 2, 5, 6, 14, 22.

13. Dana Rudhyar, *Occult Preparation for a New Age*, 262.

14. Ibid.

15. William Bennett, "America, the World, and Our Schools," presented at Ethics and Public Policy Center Conference, Washington, D.C., December 5, 1986, 9.

16. Greg Cunningham, "Blowing the Whistle on 'Global Education,'" "An internal document on the Center for Teaching International Relations," "World Citizen Curriculum" prepared for Thomas G. Tancredo, Regional Representative, U.S. Department of Education, Denver, Colorado, 1986.

17. Buehrer, *The New Age Masquerade*, 125.

18. Mel and Norma Gabler, *What Are They Teaching Our Children?* (Wheaton, Ill.: Victor Books, 1985); Berit Kjos, *Your Child and the New Age* (Wheaton, Ill.: Victor Books, 1990), 7–27; and Johanna Michaelsen, *Like Lambs to the Slaughter* (Eugene, Ore.: Harvest House Publishers, 1989). The last documents uncover scores of New Age practices in our public school systems.

CHAPTER 9: DEVELOPING CRITICAL THINKING SKILLS

1. Allan Bloom, *The Closing of the American Mind* (New York: Simon & Schuster, 1987), 19.

2. Ibid., 25.

3. Ibid., 26.

4. Bob and Gretchen Passantino, *Witch Hunt* (Nashville, Tenn.: Thomas Nelson, 1990), 85–86.

5. Ibid., 113.

6. Ibid., 117.

7. "The Fort Lauderdale Five" was comprised of Don Basham, Ern Baxter, Bob Mumford, Derek Prince, and Charles Simpson.
8. Passantino, *Witch Hunt*, 85–86.
9. Ibid.

CHAPTER 10: CULTS AND FRIENDSHIPS

1. Hannah Arendt, *The Origins of Totalitarianism* (New York: Harcourt Brace Jovanovich, 1973), 474ff.
2. Margaret T. Singer and Richard Ofshe, "Thought Reform Programs and the Production of Psychiatric Casualties," *Psychiatric Annals* 20, no. 4 (April 1990): 188–93.
3. Alfred Ells, *One Way Relationships: When You Love Them More Than They Love You* (Nashville, Tenn.: Thomas Nelson, 1990), 39. Used by permission.
4. Ibid., 58–59.
5. Ibid., 31.
6. Flavil Yeakley, Jr., *The Discipling Dilemma* (Nashville, Tenn.: Gospel Advocate Publishing, 1988), 23–28.
7. Great Commission no longer teaches this, and has acknowledged the harm this teaching caused.
8. Janis Long Harris, "How Healthy Are Your Friendships?" *Today's Christian Woman* (May/June, 1991): 44–48.
9. Stan Mooneyham, "Emotional Cloning is Never Christian," *World Vision* (February 1979), 23.
10. "Diagnostic Criteria for 301.60 Dependent Personality Disorder," in *Diagnostic and Statistical Manual of Mental Disorders, third edition, revised* (Washington, D.C., American Psychiatric Association, 1987), 354.

CHAPTER 11: CULTS AND THE CHURCH

1. Tim Stafford, "The Kingdom of the Cult Watchers," *Christianity Today* (October 7, 1991): 18–22.
2. The American Family Foundation provides a helpful "Resource List." Write to AFF, P.O. Box 2265, Bonita Springs, Fla. 33959.
3. Charles Colson, *The God of Stones and Spiders* (Wheaton, Ill.: Crossways Books, 1990), in the chapter entitled

"Friends of Religious Liberty: Why the Embarrassing Silence?"

4. Ibid., 156; Ronald Enroth, *The Lure of the Cults* (Downers Grove, Ill.: InterVarsity Press, 1987), 106–7.

5. In 1978 the United States House Subcommittee on International Organizations conducted an indepth investigation of allegations of a too-close working relationship between the Unification Church and the government of late-President Park Chung Hee for the purpose of "influencing United States foreign policy." As related by James and Marcia Rudin in their book, *Prison or Paradise? The New Religious Cults* (Philadelphia: Fortress Press, 1980), "The report called for a federal interagency task force to investigate the apparent illegal activities of the Unification Church and its many related operations. The Fraser Subcommittee cited violations of the United States tax, immigration, banking, currency, and foreign registration laws by the Unification Church." In addition, the report called for more research on cults. The full title and particulars of the report are *Final Report, "Investigation of Korean-American Relations,"* Subcommittee on International Organizations of the United States House of Representatives International Relations Committee (Washington, D.C.: United States Government Printing Office, October 31, 1978).

6. Ronald Enroth, "Why Have We Betrayed Robin?" *Christianity Today* (September 1990), 8.

7. Tim Stafford, "Kingdom," 22.

8. Ibid., 22.

9. Walter Martin, *The New Cults* (Ventura, Calif.: Vision House Publishers, rev. ed. 1980), 7.

CHAPTER 12: CULTS AND SOCIETY

1. "New Age in Business: What You and Your Employer Should Know," *SCP Newsletter* 14, no. 1 (1988): 1–6; "Business and the New Age Movement," *American Family Foundation Report* (see "Thought Reform Programs"), no date, 1–2; Richard Watring, "New Age Training in Business: Mind Control in Upper Management?" *Eternity* (February 1988): 30–32.

2. James R. Goff, Jr., "The Faith That Claims," *Christianity Today* (February 19, 1990): 16.
3. Martin Luther, *Commentary on Galatians*, Erasmus Middleton, trans., John Prince Fallowes, ed. (Grand Rapids, Mich.: Kregel Publications, 1979), 55.
4. Berkeley Rice, "Can Companies Kill?" *Psychology Today* (June 1981): 78–85; Ronald E. Yates, "Japanese Live . . . and Die . . . for Their Work," *Chicago Tribune* (November 13, 1988): 1, 14.
5. Tipper Gore, *Raising PG Kids in an X-rated Society* (Nashville: Abingdon Press, 1987).
6. Ibid., 148.
7. Allan Bloom, *The Closing of the American Mind* (New York: Simon & Schuster, 1987), 74–75.

CHAPTER 13: WHEN YOUR CHILD JOINS A CULT

1. Mary Ellen Pinkham, *How to Stop the One You Love from Drinking* (New York: G.P. Putnam's Sons, 1986), 127; see also Anonymous, "The Trouble With David," *Readers Digest* (March 1988): 161–68.
2. Carol Giambalvo, *Exit Counseling* (Chicago: Cult Awareness Network, 1990).
3. Pinkham, *How to Stop*, 134, 136.
4. The following 18 points were adapted from Carol Giambalvo's *Exit Counseling* and are used by permission.
5. This is adapted from typical statements used to get alcoholic family members to an intervention. See Pinkham, *How to Stop*, 251–64.
6. Giambalvo, *Exit Counseling*.
7. Adapted from Giambalvo, *Exit Counseling*.
8. Ibid., 41–42.

CHAPTER 14: PITFALLS TO RECOVERY

1. Madeleine Tobias, "Recovery Guidelines for Ex-members of Destructive Groups and Relationships," paper presented at conference *Recovery from Cults*, May 11–12, 1991, Philadelphia. Sponsored by the American Family Foundation, 1.
2. Ibid., 2.
3. Ibid., 1–4.

4. Cultic involvement can produce serious psychological problems, though the problems of ex-cultists may not all be cult-related. Pastors are well-advised to seek mental health consultation for severe cases.

5. Harold Busséll, "Why Evangelicals Are Attracted to the Cults," *Moody Monthly* (March 1985): 111–13.

6. In 2 Corinthians 4:2, Paul makes it clear that his own methods of evangelism were completely open and aboveboard, and thus may be used as a standard against which to compare the ministries of others. In Ephesians 5:11, he admonishes the believers at Ephesus to have nothing to do with the "unfruitful deeds of darkness, but instead even expose them"—in other words, rather than engage in underhanded deceit or other crooked behavior, the Christian is to be a person of honor and integrity, and one who brings wickedness to the light so that it might be revealed for what it is.

7. Lawrence Bennett Sullivan, Ph.D., "Counseling and Involvements in New Religious Groups," *Cultic Studies Journal* 1, no. 2 (Fall/Winter 1984): 178–95.

8. Stephen M. Ash, "A Response to Robbin's Critique of My Extremist Cult Definition and View of Cult Induced Impairment," *Cultic Studies Journal* (Fall/Winter 1984): 27–35; Paul R. Martin, "Dispelling the Myths," *Christian Research Journal* (Winter/Spring, 1989): 13.

9. Howard R. Pollio, *Behavior and Human Existence* (Monterey, Calif.: Brooks/Cole Publishing, 1982), 240.

10. Tobias, "Recovery Guidelines," 2–4. Used by permission.

11. Ibid.

12. Ibid.

13. Ronnie Janoff-Bulman, "The Aftermath of Victimization: Rebuilding Shattered Assumptions," in Charles R. Figley, Ph.D., ed., *Trauma and Its Wake: The Study and Treatment of Post-Traumatic Stress Disorder* (New York: Brunnet/Mazel Publishers, 1985), 15.

14. Ibid., 16–17.

15. Robert J. Lifton, *Thought Reform and the Psychology of Totalism* (Chapel Hill, N.C.: Univeristy of North Carolina Press, 1961, 1989).

16. Robert J. Lifton, *The Future of Immortality and Other Essays for a Nuclear Age* (New York: Basic Books, 1987), 209–20. See also Robert J. Lifton, "Cult Formation," *Cultic Studies Journal* 18, no. 1 (1991): 1–6.

17. M. J. Horowitz, "Psychological Response in Serious Life Events," in V. Hamilton and D. Warburton, ed., *Human Stress and Cognition* (New York: Wiley, 1980). See also Madeleine Tobias, "Recovery Guidelines for Examples of Destructive Groups and Relationships," 7–8.

18. Harold Busséll, *A Study of Justification, Christian Fullness, and Super Believers*, unpublished paper.

19. Dr. Walter Martin, *Essential Christianity* (Ventura, Calif.: Regal Books, 1980), 71–81.

20. Kevin Garvey, "Protecting Yourself" (from personal correspondence with the author, May 1991).

21. Jim McCotter, *Chapter Seven* (Silver Spring, Md.: Great Commission International, 1984), 40. The exact quote is: "What we call 'dating,' the Bible may call 'partiality' (James 2:9). What we call 'boyfriend/girlfriend,' the Bible may call a 'clique' or 'faction' (Galatians 5:20)."

22. "Summary of Meeting" (of ex-members of the Yarber cult), unpublished letter, Sunday, November 5, 1989.

23. James Romenesko, "The False Prophet," *Milwaukee Magazine* (March 1990): 95.

24. Ibid.

25. Ibid.

26. Marina Milligan, "Arcadia Counselor Stripped of Licenses," *Star-News* (April 30, 1989): A-8.

27. Lee Nelson, "Church Practices Revealed, Counseling Said to Include Sexual Contact," *Arcadia Highlander* (August 3, 1988): 6.

28. Lorna Goldberg and William Goldberg, "Group Work with Former Cultists," *Social Work* 27 (March 1982): 166–70; Lorna Goldberg and William Goldberg, "Short- and Long-term Effects of Cultic Involvement," presentation made at 1989 National Cult Awareness Network Conference, Pittsburgh, Pennsylvania, November 1989.

APPENDIX A:
RESOURCES AND
ORGANIZATIONS

The following are a few cult research and information organizations, some of which publish newsletters, magazines, or journals on cults. Also included are organizations that offer counseling assistance. Please offer any financial support you can to organizations in this appendix; counter-cult ministries and organizations are notoriously underfunded and need all the help they can get.

American Family Foundation
P.O. Box 336
Weston, MA 02193
212-249-7693

Director: Michael D. Langone

Provides information on a wide variety of cults. Publishes the scholarly *Cultic Studies Journal* and *The Cult Observer*, a review of media coverage of cults.

Answers in Action
P.O. Box 2067
Costa Mesa, CA 92628
714-957-0249

Directors: Robert and Gretchen Passantino

Apologetic Research Coalition
P.O. Box 168
Trenton, MI 48183
313-562-4600

Director: Keith E. Tolbert

Bethel Ministries
P.O. Box 3818
Manhattan Beach, CA 90266
213-545-7831

Director: Randall Watters

Publishes *The Bethel Ministries Newsletter*, reporting news and analyses of Jehovah's Witnesses teachings and activities.

Bethesda PsycHealth System/ Institute for Ritualistic Deviant Behavior
4400 E. Cliff Ave.
Denver, CO 80222
303-759-6040

Chief Pastoral Officer:
Wayne A. Van Kampen

An in-patient facility providing therapy for those affected by occult/satanic involvement. Also publishes the *Bethesda PsycHealth Reporter*, dealing with Satanism and ritual abuse.

Biblical Evangelist
PO Drawer 940
Ingleside, TX 78362
512-776-2767

Director: Robert L. Sumner

Publishes *The Biblical Evangelist*, provides literature on various cults.

Bob Larson Ministries
P.O. Box 36480
Denver, CO 80236
303-980-1511

Director: Bob Larson

Bothered About Dungeons and Dragons
P.O. Box 5513
Richmond, VA 23220
804-264-0403

Director: Pat Pulling

Specializes in fantasy role-playing games, ritualistic crime involving black magic, and any harmful influences on children which lead to ritualistic crime.

Cheyenne Mesa
1303 S. 8th St.
Colorado Springs, CO 80906
719-520-1400

Director: Michael Forgy

Offers counseling and other services for victims of satanic ritual abuse, and others who have had prior involvement with Satanism.

Christian Apologetics: Research and Information Service (CARIS)
P.O. Box 1659
Milwaukee, WI 53201
414-771-7379

Director: Jim Valentine

Christian Ministries International (CMI)
7601 Superior Terr.
Eden Prairie, MN 55344
612-937-8424

Christian Research Institute (CRI)
P.O. Box 500
San Juan Capistrano, CA 92693
714-855-9926

Director: Hank Hannegraf

Provides information on a wide variety of cults and cultic organizations, especially Bible-based groups. Publishes *The Christian Research Journal* and *The Christian Research Newsletter*.

Christian Way International, Inc.
P.O. Box 1675
Lancaster, CA 93539
805-948-8308

Director: Carolyn Poole

Emphasis on Christian Science and New Thought groups.

Commission on Cults and Missionaries
Community Relations Committee
Jewish Federation Council of Greater Los Angeles
6505 Wilshire Blvd., #802
Los Angeles, CA 90048
213-852-1234, ext. 2813

Director: Rachel Andres

Cornerstone Press
4707 N. Malden
Chicago, IL 60640
312-989-2080

Publishes Directory of Cult Research Organizations.

Criminal Justice Technical Services
P.O. Box 309
Tiffin, OH 44883
419-447-8611

Director: Dale W. Griffis, Ph.D., *former police captain in Tiffin, Ohio.*

Specializes in Satanism, witchcraft, and the occult.

C.S.R.A.
P.O. Box 48451
Wichita, KS 67201

Director: Deborah Rolof

A support group for survivors of ritualistic abuse.

Cult Awareness Network
2421 W. Pratt Blvd., #1173
Chicago, IL 60645
312-267-7777

Director: Cynthia Kisser

Affiliates around the United States. Provides information on a wide variety of cults. Publishes a monthly newsletter, *The Cult Awareness Network News.*

Cult Hot-Line and Clinic
1651 Third Ave.
New York, NY 10028
212-860-8533

Cult Information Service
1541 Northcrest Ave.
Columbus, OH 43220
614-459-0634

Director: Bill Lewis

**Eastern Christian Outreach
(ECHO)**
5909 Elmhurst St.
Philadelphia, PA 19149
215-289-8715

Provides tapes and literature, counseling, and ex-member support.

Dr. Ronald M. Enroth
Westmont College
955 La Paz Road
Santa Barbara, CA 93108
805-969-5051

Academic research and writing, especially from a sociological perspective.

Evangelical Ministries to New Religions
P.O. Box 409090
Chicago, IL 60640-9090
312-989-2088

Executive Director: Eric Pement

An umbrella organization for evangelical cultwatch ministries. Publishes a newsletter.

Ex-Mormons and Concerned Christians
P.O. Box 542
Okemos, MI 48805
517-655-3797

Director: S. L. Douglas

FOCUS
CAN National Office
2421 West Pratt Blvd., Suite

1173
Chicago, IL 60645
312-267-7777

National Coordinator,
Nancy Miquelon:
303-945-5961

Support group for ex-cult members.

Free Minds, Inc.
P.O. Box 4216
Minneapolis, MN 55414
612-378-2528

Free the Masons Ministries
P.O. Box 1077
Issaquah, WA 98027

Frontline Ministries
P.O. Box 1100
La Canada Flintridge, CA 91012
818-794-5849

Director: Wally Tope

William and Lorna Goldberg
302 Van Saun Drive
River Edge, NJ 07661
201-488-8787

Ex-cult member counseling.

Hartgrove Hospital
520 N. Ridgeway Avenue
Chicago, IL 60624
312-722-3113

Program Consultant: Dale B. Trahan
Community Relations Representative: Beth Vargo

Hartgrove Hospital is a center for the treatment of

ritualistic deviant behavior as typical of occult/satanic involvement.

His Mansion
Box 40
Hillsboro, NH 03244
603-464-5555

Director: Stan Farmer

A residential center specializing in counseling youth troubled in the areas of drugs, alcohol, delinquency, teen pregnancy, and the occult.

Home Mission Board, Southern Baptist Convention
Interfaith Witness Dept.
1350 Spring St., N.W.
Atlanta, GA 30367
404-898-7000

Director: Gary Leazer

HRT Ministries, Inc.
P.O. Box 12
Newtonville, NY 12128

Director: Harmon R. Taylor

Provides information on Freemasonry.

Incest Survivors Resource Network, Inc.
15 Rutherford Place
New York, NY 10003
513-935-3031

An agency offering information on incest and ritual abuse.

Institute of Contemporary Christianity
P.O. Box A
Oakland, NJ 07436

Director: James Bjornstad

Interfaith Coalition of Concern About the Cults
711 Third Ave., 12th Floor
New York, NY 10017

Director: Philip Abramowitz

International Cult Education Program (ICEP)
P.O. Box 1232, Gracie Station
New York, NY 10028
212-439-1550

Director: Marcia R. Rudin

A cooperative program of the Cult Awareness Network and the American Family Foundation. Publishes *Young People and Cults.*

J.O.E.L. Ministries
P.O. Box 12638
El Paso, TX 79913

An arm of W.A.T.C.H. Network. Works with teenagers coming out of the occult and drugs.

Jude 3 Missions
P.O. Box 1901
Orange, CA 92668
714-972-1878

Kurt and Cindy Van Gordon

Emphasis on Mormonism and Jehovah's Witnesses.

Lutheran Church—Missouri Synod
Commission on
Organizations
1333 S. Kirkwood Rd.
St. Louis, MO 63122
314-965-9000, ext. 227

Director: Philip Lochhaas

The Master's College
Dept. of Apologetics
P.O. Box 878
Newhall, CA 91322
805-259-3540

Professor Edmund C. Gruss

Information especially on Jehovah's Witnesses.

Michael Paul & Associates
P.O. Box 1168
Crockett, TX 75835
409-544-4953

Directors: Michael Haynes and Paul Carlin

Offers seminars on the occult; serves as consultant to law enforcement agencies.

Missionary Crusader
2451 34th St.
Lubbock, TX 79411
806-799-1040

Director: Homer Duncan

Books and tracts on major cults.

Mormon Studies
P.O. Box 1091
Webster, NY 14580
716-872-4033

Directors: John and Phyllis Farkas

Mormonism Research Ministry
P.O. Box 20705
El Cajon, CA 92021
619-447-3873

Director: Bill McKeever

Publishes a quarterly magazine, *Mormonism Researched.*

Mount Carmel Outreach
P.O. Box 5761
Rockford, IL 61125-0761
815-968-CULT

Director: Kevin Johnson

Branches in other cities in Illinois and nearby states.

New Directions Ministries
P.O. Box 2347
Burlington, NC 27216
919-227-1273

Director: J.L. Williams

Information on cults in general, the occult and The Way International specifically.

Personal Freedom Outreach
P.O. Box 26062
St. Louis, MO 63136
314-388-2648

Director: M. Kurt Goedelman

General cult information; publishes *The Quarterly Journal*, a magazine with well-researched articles

on cult-related topics.
Branches in other cities also.

Probe Ministries International
1900 Firman Dr., Suite 100
Richardson, TX 75081
214-480-0240

Administrative Director: Ray Cotton

Carl Raschke, Ph.D.
P.O. Box 783
Monument, CO 80132
303-869-6141

Dr. Raschke, a professor of religion at the University of Denver, has researched and written extensively on cults, especially in the field of the occult, witchcraft, and Satanism.

Saints Alive in Jesus (International HQ)
P.O. Box 1076
Issaquah, WA 98027
206-392-2077

Director: Ed Decker

Sound Doctrine Ministries
P.O. Box 1962
Exeter, NH 03833
603-772-3093

Director: Steven Tsoukalis

Spirit of Truth Ministry
P.O. Box 6986
Los Osos, CA 93412
805-528-6863

Directors: Judith and Edward Matta

Emphasis on Word-Faith ("Positive Confession") Movement.

Spiritual Counterfeits Project
P.O. Box 4308
Berkeley, CA 94704
415-540-0300

Director: Tal Brooke

Provides information and counseling on a wide variety of cults with special emphasis on Eastern/mystical cults. Publishes *The Spiritual Counterfeits Project Newsletter* and the *SCP Journal.*

Task Force on Missionaries & Cults
Jewish Community Relations Council of New York
111 West 40th St.
New York, NY 10018
212-860-8533

The Teaching Ministry
P.O. Box 22596
Fort Worth, TX 76122

Director: Mark Stepherson

Seminars on Mormonism and Jehovah's Witnesses.

Moshe Torem, M.D.
400 Wabash Ave.
Akron, OH 44307
216-384-6525

Dr. Torem specializes in treating victims of ritualistic abuse and Multiple Personality Disorder.

Utah Christian Publications
P.O. Box 1884
Salt Lake City, UT 84110

Directors: Jerald and Sandra Tanner

Produces some of the best literature on Mormonism.

Utah Missions, Inc.
P.O. Box 348
Marlow, OK 73055
800-654-3992

Director: John L. Smith

Literature on Mormonism, especially on how to witness to Mormons using the Book of Mormon itself. Publishes *The Evangel*, monthly newspaper.

W.A.T.C.H. Network
P.O. Box 12638
El Paso, TX 79913
915-581-2011

Director: Sue Joyner

Information and services for those involved in witchcraft and Satanism and trying to get out.

Watchman Fellowship
P.O. Box 7681
Columbus, GA 31908
404-576-4321

Director: David Henke

Branches in other cities also. Information mainly on Mormonism, Jehovah's Witnesses, and New Age Movement. Publishes the *Watchman Expositor*.

Tom Wedge
P.O. Box 428
Bellefontaine, OH 43311
614-267-2380

Specializes in Satanism, witchcraft, and the occult.

Wellspring Retreat and Resource Center
P.O. Box 67
Albany, OH 45710
614-698-6277

Director: Dr. Paul R. Martin

Provides post-cult rehabilitative counseling in a residential facility. Offers both psychological counseling by a licensed Christian counselor (Dr. Martin) as well as theological studies with trained instructors. Publishes a quarterly newsletter, *The Wellspring Messenger*.

West Central Georgia Regional Hospital Division of Mental Health, Mental Retardation, & Substance Abuse
3000 Schatulga Road
P.O. Box 12435
Columbus, GA 31995-7499
404-568-5154

Offers treatment for victims of ritualistic abuse and occult involvement.

Witness, Inc.
P.O. Box 597
Clayton, CA 94517
415-672-5979

Director: Duane Magnani

Provides information especially on Jehovah's Witnesses and Mormonism.

CANADIAN RESOURCES

Contemporary Religious Movements Resource Center
c/o Winnipeg Bible College and Theological Seminary
Otterburne, MB R0A 1G0

Director: Wendy Peterson

Cult Information Centre
c/o Jewish Community Centre
151 Chapel Street
Ottawa, ON K1N 7Y2

Info-Cult
3460 Stanley St.
Montreal, QC H3A 1R8
514-845-9171

Director: Michael Kropveld

Manitoba Cult Awareness Centre, Inc.
P.O. Box 31 Norwood Grove
Winnipeg, MB R2H 3B8
204-474-1201

No Longer Children Support Group Assn.
P.O. Box 415
8155 Park Road
Richmond, BC V6Y 3C9

Directors: David and Mary Lou Hiebert

A support group for ex-members of the Children of God cult. Publishes a newsletter as funds permit.

Saskatchewan Citizens Against Mind Control, Inc. (SCAMC)
P.O. Box 74
Saskatoon, SK S7K 3K1
306-9660-8500

Society Against Mind Abuse
P.O. Box 5024
Postal Station E
Edmonton, AB T5B 4C1

APPENDIX B:
HELPFUL CURRICULUM

Here are some excellent training materials and resource organizations to help in your information gathering and question asking.

Seeking Information: Parts I & II, by Brant W. Abrahamson (published by The Teachers Press, 3731 Madison Ave., Brookfield, IL 60513 at $29). This curriculum was designed to be taught in secondary and post-secondary schools over a six- to nine-week period by teachers at the Brookfield High School in Brookfield, Illinois. The curriculum focuses on critical thinking and evaluation of information, with an analysis of freedom and authority. It includes sections on cults, occultism, psychic phenomena, world religions, folk wisdom, humanities, and the sciences. The parts include the student text, discussion guide, and teacher's manual. It can be used in colleges, churches, and abridged for shorter teaching sessions.

Cultivating Cult-Evading by Dr. Sandy Andron (Central Agency for Jewish Education, 4200 Biscayne Boulevard, Miami, FL 33137). This helpful forty-four-page book includes the basics about cultism, including definitions of a cult, the dynamics of joining a cult, the processes of being in a cult, and specific steps to talk through the cult problem. Useful for schools and churches.

International Cult Education Program (P.O. Box 132, Gracie Station, New York, NY 10028). ICEP comprises both professional and lay experts involved in cult education in schools, churches, synagogues, and colleges. ICEP is a joint program of The American

Family Foundation and the Cult Awareness Network. Participating organizations are the National Association of Student Personnel Administrators and the Association for College Unions-International. They publish a monthly newsletter called *Young People and Cults,* and have produced an excellent video presentation on the cult phenomenon entitled "Cults: Saying No Under Pressure," narrated by Charlton Heston.

Impact: Improve Minimal Proficiences by Activating Critical Thinking (21412 Magnolia St., Huntington Beach, CA 92642 (714) 964-3106). Impact is an introductory program in critical thinking. It presents a broad-based instructional approach to this area which helps teachers and administrators introduce skills to their peers as well as their students. Impact's strongest feature is that it does not approach critical thinking as a separate subject but infuses the critical thinking skills into the established curriculum.

APPENDIX C:
RECOMMENDED READING

General Works

Andres, Rachel, and James R. Lane, eds. *Cults and Consequences: The Definitive Handbook.* Los Angeles: Commission on Cults and Missionaries, Community Relations Committee, Jewish Federation Council of Greater Los Angeles, 1988. Contains helpful articles on a number of important topics relevant to the cult problem, including information for parents of cult members and discussions of various aspects of the recovery process.

Ankerberg, John, and John Weldon. *Cult Watch: What You Need to Know About Spiritual Deception.* Eugene, OR: Harvest House, 1991. This is a substantial book that "provides historical background and the vital facts on the major beliefs of modern religious movements and looks closely at the reasons people become entrapped in them." Major divisions are: Mormonism, Jehovah's Witnesses, The Masonic Lodge, The New Age Movement, Spirit Guides, Astrology, The Occult, and False Teaching in the Church.

Braswell, George W., Jr. *Understanding Sectarian Groups in America.* Nashville: Broadman, 1986. The author, professor of missions and world religions at Southeastern Baptist Theological Seminary, offers thorough analyses of Mormonism, Jehovah's Witnesses, the Unification Church, and the Way International, and briefer summaries of several other sects and cults, from the Worldwide Church of God and the "local church" of Witness Lee to witchcraft, Satanism, the

Hare Krishnas, and other Eastern cults. Includes some groups not often found discussed elsewhere.

Breese, Dave. *Know the Marks of Cults.* Wheaton, IL: Scripture Press, 1975, 1988. This book enables the reader to identify cultic churches and organizations by measuring them against twelve distinguishing characteristics, thus largely eliminating the need to be familiar with all of the estimated 3,000 to 5,000 cults in America today. Highly recommended.

Busséll, Harold. *Unholy Devotion: Why Cults Lure Christians.* Grand Rapids: Zondervan, 1983. Working from the premise that "the lure of the cults is not doctrine, but style" and "not reasoned faith, but the promise of a better life," Busséll demonstrates that "many evangelical youth are drawn to cults because too often the marks of spirituality they set forth uncannily resemble the qualities we exhibit in our Christian churches," namely, an overemphasis on subjective religious experience, a confusion of the Gospel with our response to the Gospel, a tendency to spiritualize issues to justify our actions, evaluating leaders on their ability to sway us emotionally, and a failure to encourage critical thinking. Highly recommended. (Though currently out of print, it is worth the effort to look for it.)

Enroth, Ronald M. *Evangelizing the Cults.* Ann Arbor, MI: Servant, 1990.

_____. *The Lure of the Cults and New Religions: Why They Attract and What We Can Do.* Rev. ed. Downers Grove, IL: InterVarsity Press, 1979, 1987. An excellent book by a well-known Christian cult watcher and professor of sociology at Westmont College in California. Describes sociological aspects of cultic phenomena, especially the dynamics of such groups that attracts individuals, holds them as members, and ultimately harms them spiritually, psychologically, and often physically.

Enroth, Ronald M., et al. *A Guide to Cults and New Religions.* Downers Grove, IL: InterVarsity Press, 1983. Provides detailed analyses of ten major newer cults, including The Way International, Eckankar, Transcendental Meditation, and the Unification Church.

Enroth, Ronald M., and J. Gordon Melton. *Why Cults Succeed Where the Church Fails.* Elgin, IL: Brethren Press, 1985. Based on an interview with the authors published in

Christianity Today, this book is in the form of a dialogue between Enroth, Melton, and the interviewer on the important questions of why cults seem so often to be more attractive to young people than the church is, whether cults actually harm their members or even sometimes help them, and how Christians should respond to the cults.

Giambalvo, Carol. *Exit Counseling.* Weston, MA: American Family Foundation, 1992. This is the "standard" for the exit counseling process.

Hassan, Steve. *Combatting Cult Mind Control.* Rochester, VT: Park Street Press, 1990. A must! The definitive book on cult mind control.

Howard, Jay, with Timothy Fink and Nathan Unseth. *Confronting the Cultist in the New Age.* Old Tappan, NJ: Revell, 1990.

LeBar, Rev. James J. *Cults, Sects, and the New Age.* Huntington, IN: Our Sunday Visitor, 1989. Written by the chief cult researcher of the New York Diocese of the Roman Catholic Church, this book contains helpful information on a variety of American cults, including the "shepherding/discipleship" error. The latter focuses on the Boston Church of Christ movement and the Catholic charismatic Word of God community of Ann Arbor, Mich., prior to recent reforms and a split in the movement.

Martin, Walter R. *The Kingdom of the Cults.* Minneapolis: Bethany, 1977, 1985. The classic study of religious cults by the late founder and director of the Christian Research Institute. Deals with the older, established cults of Mormonism, Jehovah's Witnesses, Christian Science, etc., but also with less well-known cults like Theosophy, Bahá'í, and Spiritism, as well as with newer cults such as the Worldwide Church of God, Scientology, and the Unification Church. Includes extremely helpful chapters on "Scaling the Language Barrier," "The Psychological Structure of Cultism," "The Jesus of the Cults," and "The Road to Recovery."

McDowell, Josh, and Don Stewart. *Handbook of Today's Religions.* San Bernardino, CA: Campus Crusade for Christ, 1983. "A clear, concise reference work. Practical insights into the background, organization, and beliefs of today's cults, occult, secular and non-Christian religions. Comprehensive glossary and up-to-date bibliographies for further reading."

Passantino, Robert and Gretchen. *Answers to the Cultist at Your Door*. Eugene, OR: Harvest House, 1981. "A clear, concise, step-by-step guide to answering the questionable doctrines of cultists." If you want to know how to respond to that Jehovah's Witness standing at your door, this is a good book for you. Also includes testimonies of ex-cultists, and information on how to help loved ones in cults.

Rudin, James and Marcia. *Prison or Paradise? The New Religious Cults*. Philadelphia: Fortress, 1980. The authors are leading Jewish cult experts. James is a rabbi and National Director of Interreligious Affairs of the American Jewish Committee, and Marcia is director of the International Cult Education Program. Theirs is one of the best overall books on the cult problem, discussing the questions of who joins and why, how today's cults are different from older religious movements, how dangerous modern cults are, and how to counter the cults. Also includes brief descriptions of several of the newer cults, including some not usually dealt with in other books, like the Tony and Susan Alamo Christian Foundation, the Church of Armageddon/Love Family, and the Body of Christ.

Sire, James. *Scripture Twisting: 20 Ways the Cults Misread the Bible*. Downers Grove, IL: InterVarsity Press, 1980. An extremely important book discussing common errors committed by cults in their (mis)use of the Bible. A book that anyone concerned about handling the Word of God accurately should read and heed.

Tucker, Ruth. *Another Gospel: Alternate Religions and the New Age Movement*. Grand Rapids: Zondervan, 1989. A thorough and well-researched book dealing with the major historical cults as well as many of the newer ones. Extensive footnotes and bibliography direct the reader who wishes more in-depth study.

Watson, William. *A Concise Dictionary of Cults and Religions*. Chicago: Moody Press, 1991. One of the best source books for brief information on cults and new religions. Includes much information difficult to find elsewhere, including many little-known cults that don't often make the news.

Appendix C

The Children of God

Davis, Deborah (Linda Berg), with Bill Davis. *The Children of God: The Inside Story.* Grand Rapids: Zondervan, 1984. Written by the elder daughter of Children of God founder David (Moses David) Berg, this is a shockingly honest and revealing look behind the scenes of the cult and the life of the author's father. Includes the dramatic story of the Deborah's awakening to the errors of the group and her escape to spiritual freedom in Christ.

Gordon, Ruth. *Children of Darkness.* Wheaton, IL: Tyndale House, 1988. An ex-member of the cult describes her odyssey, from her joining the group in 1975, living with the COG in South America, and marrying a member of the group, to her exit five years later and the struggle she and her children went through in readjusting to life outside the cult.

Jehovah's Witnesses

Ankerberg, John, and John Weldon. *The Facts on Jehovah's Witnesses.* Eugene, OR: Harvest House, 1988. "Answers to the 30 most frequently asked questions about the Watchtower Society." Included as a chapter in the authors' book, *Cult Watch.*

Bowman, Robert M., Jr. *Jehovah's Witnesses, Jesus Christ, and the Gospel of John.* Grand Rapids: Baker, 1988. "Uses John 1:1 and 8:58 to refute errors made by Jehovah's Witnesses."

Martin, Walter, and Norman Klann. *Jehovah of the Watchtower.* Minneapolis: Bethany House, 1981. "This book is a must for every library. It is one of the most comprehensive books on the subject and has gone through a number of revisions, with its present content doubling the original material."

Mormonism

Ahmanson, John, translated by Gleason L. Archer. *Secret History: An Eyewitness Account of the Rise of Mormonism.* Chicago: Moody Press, 1984. "Written in Danish in 1876, *Secret History* examines the rise and spread of Mormonism in the United States through the eyes of a disillusioned Mormon."

Anderson, Einar. *Inside Story of Mormonism.* Grand Rapids: Kregel, 1973, 1974. "Here is an opportunity to read first-hand the problems involved with Mormonism from a man who has spent his life grappling with these problems. . . .Mr. Anderson compares here the power, the prestige, the historic authenticity and infallibility of the Bible with the official books of Mormonism." Thoroughly documents little-known and sometimes shocking aspects of Mormon history.

Tanner, Jerald and Sandra. *The Changing World of Mormonism.* Chicago: Moody Press, 1980, 1981. At 592 pages, an abridgement of the authors' "magnum opus," *Mormonism— Shadow or Reality?* "a landmark work exposing the weaknesses, fallacies, and corruptions of the Mormon church." This book "is a thorough investigation of the history of Mormon leaders and changes in doctrine and practice." Contains many pages of photocopies from Mormon publications which verify the authors' revelations. Includes what is possibly the most extensive bibliography currently in print of books on Mormonism.

The New Age Movement
(Based in part on bibliographical divisions in Elliot Miller, *A Crash Course in the New Age Movement.*)

A. General Works

Ankerberg, John, and John Weldon. *The Facts on the New Age Movement: Answers to 30 Most Asked Questions about the New Age Movement.* Eugene, OR: Harvest House, 1988. Included as a chapter in the authors' book, *Cult Watch.*

Chandler, Russell. *Understanding the New Age.* Grand Rapids: Zondervan, 1988. "Explores every facet of the New Age movement, featuring interviews with more than thirty proponents and critics."

Groothuis, Douglas R. *Confronting the New Age.* Downers Grove, IL: InterVarsity Press, 1988. "How to resist this growing religious movement, identify its concepts, discuss them with understanding, and combat it evangelistically."

———. *Revealing the New Age Jesus.* Downers Grove, IL: InterVarsity Press, 1989. Discusses the various ways New Age proponents distort the biblical teaching about Jesus Christ, and refutes these distortions with clear biblical exposition.

Hoyt, Karen, J., Isamu Yamamoto, and the Spiritual Counterfeits Project. *The New Age Rage: A Probing Analysis of the Newest Religious Craze.* Old Tappan, NJ: Revell, 1987. "In eleven chapters, a group of authorities in various fields discuss the [New Age] movement from their unique perspectives. They explore its impact on medicine, science, politics, psychology, sex, and more. In a cohesive, sensible fashion, the authors emphasize the importance of understanding and combatting the negative ideas represented in these loosely linked movements."

Larson, Bob. *Straight Answers on the New Age.* Nashville: Thomas Nelson, 1989. "Describes terms, names, and titles associated with the New Age movement, which most of us tend to naively accept as harmless."

Martin, Walter. *The New Age Cult.* Minneapolis: Bethany House, 1989. The last book from the pen of the late founder and director of the Christian Research Institute, this is an able exposé and refutation of major beliefs and practices of the New Age Movement.

Miller, Elliot. *A Crash Course in the New Age Movement.* Grand Rapids: Baker, 1989. "Miller does an 'inside out' probe of the New Age mindset. He was converted from New Age spirituality to Christ. He surveys and critiques New Age ideology, tracks down the so-called Aquarian conspiracy, and explores the New Age in the context of Christian eschatology." All in all, one of the very best and most complete evangelical discussions of the New Age Movement.

B. Books on Reincarnation

Albrecht, Mark C. *Reincarnation, a Christian Critique of a New Age Doctrine.* Downers Grove, IL: InterVarsity Press, 1982. A careful examination of reincarnation and related matters, "looking especially at the case for and against spontaneous recall and regression to past lives. He offers readers a clear biblical assessment of this New Age doctrine." Examines the question of whether the Bible supports the idea of reincarnation, contrasts Eastern and Western worldviews, and discusses philosophical, moral, and theological objections to reincarnation.

Morey, Robert A. *Reincarnation and Christianity: Has the Traditional Viewpoint of the Church Been Lost?* Minneapolis: Bethany House, 1980.

Rawlings, Maurice S., M.D. *Life Wish: Reincarnation: Reality or Hoax?* Nashville: Thomas Nelson, 1981. The author "explores why so many people have begun to take reincarnation seriously and compares it with the teachings of the Bible. He concludes that the two are neither compatible nor reconcilable. Moreover, he warns that trying to mix the two beliefs can lead a person far away from true Christianity."

C. Eastern Mysticism and the New Age Movement

Brooke, Tal. *Riders of the Cosmic Circuit: Rajneesh, Sai Baba, Muktananda . . . Gods of the New Age.* Batavia, IL: Lion, 1986. The author once "held a privileged position in the inner circle of Sai Baba devotees in India. This experience also helped him gain the confidence of members of the Rajneesh ashram in India." Brooke shows that the essence of the leading gurus "is not a new teaching but a new consciousness."

Muck, Terry. *Alien Gods on American Turf.* Wheaton, IL: Scripture Press, Victor Books. Describes how "world religions are evangelizing your neighborhood."

D. New Age Medicine and Holistic Health

Matzat, Don. *Inner Healing.* Eugene, OR: Harvest House, 1987. "Amid a barrage of conflicting opinions [regarding holistic health], Don Matzat offers a careful and thoughtful investigation of the issues involved in inner healing. In this sound presentation, every concerned Christian will be helped to sort through the differing perspectives and arrive at a truly biblical understanding of the healing that only God can provide."

Reisser, Paul C., Teri K. Reisser, and John Weldon. *New Age Medicine: A Christian Perspective on Holistic Health.* Downers Grove, IL: InterVarsity Press, 1987. "A Christian perspective on holistic health. Explains methods like therapeutic touch, biofeedback, homeopathy, and psychic healing."

The Occult, Satanism, and Witchcraft

Gore, Tipper. *Raising PG Kids in an X-Rated Society.* Nashville: Abingdon Press, 1987.

Johnston, Jerry. *The Edge of Evil: The Rise of Satanism in North America.* Dallas: Word, Inc., 1989. "Warns us of the rise of

Satanism in America. Describes the warning signs of involvement in the occult," and offers suggestions on how to reach those (especially teens) involved in it. Thoroughly researched through numerous interviews with law enforcement officials and other investigators into Satanism, as well as with several former practitioners currently incarcerated because of crimes committed in the name of Satan. Discusses the lure of the occult, the various branches of the occult, and the question of whether the Satan worshipped is a real being or something else.

Kahaner, Larry. *Cults That Kill: Probing the Underworld of Occult Crime.* New York: Warner Books, 1988. "Based on probing interviews and exhaustive research, *Cults That Kill* tears the shroud off the most explosive issue in law enforcement today." The author includes extensive quotes from police officers engaged on "the front lines in the war against occult crime." He cites "the testimony of experts, followers of white and black [magical] arts, and victims." Not for the squeamish.

Korem, Dan. *Powers.* Downers Grove, IL: InterVarsity Press, 1988. "A professional magician unravels the mystery of paranormal activity. He exposes psychic 'cold reading,' telekinesis, and psychic detectives and takes a fresh look at old claims about Jesus' resurrection."

Langone, Michael D., Ph.D., and Linda O. Blood. *Satanism and Occult-Related Violence: What You Should Know.* Weston, MA: The American Family Foundation, 1990. "This important, thoroughly documented report provides a balanced overview of the problems posed by the recent upsurge of Satanism and occult-related violence in the United States." Relates several infamous cases of Satanic crime, offers a brief summary of the history of Satanism, describes several specific Satanic cults, distinguishes three occult folk religions that have appeared in the United States, explores the attraction of Satanism to our young people, and suggests some very helpful and practical steps parents and other concerned citizens can take to counter this very real menace.

Larson, Bob. *Satanism: The Seduction of America's Youth.* Nashville: Thomas Nelson, 1989. "Examines the pervasive influence of satanic activity on youth. . . . Provides practical ways to recognize and combat Satanism."

McDowell, Josh, and Don Stewart. *Demons, Witches, and the Occult*. Wheaton, IL: Tyndale House, 1983, 1988.

———. *The Occult*. San Bernardino, CA: Here's Life, 1982, revised and updated 1992.

Passantino, Bob and Gretchen. *When the Devil Dares Your Kids*. Ann Arbor, MI: Servant, 1991. A well-researched and thoroughly documented examination of the growing menace of Satanism, witchcraft, and the occult, and their attraction to many of today's young people. This is "a balanced and biblically-based resource—a book that may save your child from entrapment in the occult."

Phillips, Phil. *Turmoil in the Toybox*. Lancaster, PA: Starburst, 1986. "A shocking exposé of the toy and cartoon industry."

Raschke, Carl A. *Painted Black*. San Francisco: Harper & Row, 1990. An in-depth look into the world of the occult and Satanism by a professor of religion at the University of Denver.

Wedge, Thomas, with Robert L. Powers. *The Satan Hunter*. Canton, OH: Daring Books, 1988. Provides a summary of the history of Satanism, a description of the black mass, a discussion of the relationship between heavy metal rock music and fantasy role-playing games with Satanism and the occult, and explains the differences between traditional and nontraditional Satanism. Begins with a detailed account of the case of Sean Sellers, the sixteen-year-old from Oklahoma City who murdered his parents as a sacrifice to Satan. Also includes discussions of santeria and paganism, and several pages depicting occult signs and symbols and explaining occult terminology.

The Church of Scientology

Atack, Jon. *A Piece of the Blue Sky: Scientology, Dianetics, and L. Ron Hubbard Exposed*. New York: Carol, 1990. Written by a former nine-year member of the Church of Scientology, this book "exposes [L. Ron] Hubbard's bizarre imagination and behavior throughout his life and traces the creation of Scientology in the years following World War II to perhaps the final schism following Hubbard's death in 1986. The abuses, contradictions, falsehoods, paranoia and greed of Hubbard and some of his pseudo-military Scientologist henchman are now finally told." Includes extremely meticulous documentation in several pages of end-notes, bibliography, and index.

Corydon, Bent. *L. Ron Hubbard, Messiah or Madman?* Revised, expanded, and updated edition Fort Lee, NJ: Barricade Books Inc., 1992. Offers a detailed history of L. Ron Hubbard and the Church of Scientology, demonstrating Hubbard's penchant for reinventing his life story, and otherwise playing fast-and-loose with historical facts. Describes Hubbard's early involvement with practitioners of black magic as well as his careless attitude with regard to his marriage vows. Includes a glossary of Scientological terms and eight pages of black-and-white photographs.

Miller, Russell. *Bare Faced Messiah: The True Story of L. Ron Hubbard.* New York: Henry Holt, 1988. Now difficult to obtain in the U.S. due to a Scientology lawsuit against the author, this book is (like the previous two listings) a thorough exposé of L. Ron Hubbard and his Church of Scientology. Well worth looking for (may be available from the Cult Awareness Network; see address in Appendix A).

Totalist Aberrant Christian Organizations ("Shepherding/Discipleship Groups")

Arterburn, Stephen, and Jack Felton. *Toxic Faith: Understanding and Overcoming Religious Addiction.* Nashville: Thomas Nelson, 1991. "Arterburn and Felton distinguish healthy faith from misguided religiosity and provide the balance between the destructive extremes of being dependent or being independent. They point the way to recovery with a step-by-step process of redefining your understanding of God and religion, rebuilding your relationship with God, and repairing family relationships."

Assemblies of God General Presbytery. *The Discipleship and Submission Movement.* Springfield, MO: Assemblies of God Publishing House, 1976. This pamphlet consists of "the report of the committee [of the Assemblies of God] to study the discipleship and submission movement." It is a very helpful evaluation of the movement and its errors from a sound biblical perspective.

Barron, Bruce. *If You Really Want to Follow Jesus.* Sycamore, IL: Partners Press, 1981. A firsthand examination and critique of the so-called "covenant community" movement, especially as exemplified by the Work of Christ community in Lansing, Michigan, an "ecumenical charismatic community of Catholic origin" associated with the Sword of the Spirit network created by the Word of God community in Ann Arbor, Michigan. The author focuses on the sometimes serious difficulties caused by an unbiblically authoritarian style of leadership (confessed and repented of two years ago by several leaders, but not by others, leading to a split in the movement).

Barrs, Jerram. *Shepherds and Sheep: A Biblical View of Leading and Following.* Downers Grove, IL: InterVarsity Press, 1983. Regrettably now out of print, this book is an extremely helpful discussion of the biblical teaching on authority and submission, with an analysis of various common extremes fostered by spiritually abusive churches.

Enroth, Ronald M. *Churches That Abuse.* Grand Rapids: Zondervan, 1992. Suggesting ten common characteristics of abusive churches, Enroth offers clear descriptions of how these are manifested, and the often devastating effects they can have, by relating the true stories of numerous ex-members of such groups. The author names many of these churches, but even more helpfully gives guidelines to enable the reader to discern problems in *any* church or organization and to recognize when his own church may begin drifting toward the fringe.

Johnson, David, and Jeff VanVonderen. *The Subtle Power of Spiritual Abuse.* Minneapolis: Bethany House, 1991. An extremely timely book that details the many forms of spiritual abuse. The authors elaborate the subjects of "Spiritual Abuse and Its Victims," "Abusive Leaders and Why They Are Trapped," and "Post-Abuse Recovery." Highly recommended.

Jones, Jerry. *What Does the Boston Movement Teach?* (Two Volumes). Bridgeton, MO: Mid-America Book and Tape Sales, 1990. With the use of numerous photocopies of newsletters, church bulletins, and other material produced by the Boston Church of Christ, as well as a large number of letters, newspaper, and magazine articles, and analyses of the movement by its critics and former members, Jones evaluates this fast-growing and highly controversial movement, detailing many of its errors and dangers in the light of

Scripture. Jones writes as a former elder of the Boston Church of Christ and current leader in the mainline Churches of Christ.

Yeakley, Flavil. *The Discipling Dilemma*. Nashville: Gospel Advocate, 1988. One of the very best analyses of the Boston Church of Christ movement, its unbiblical teachings and practices, and the potential and actual harm to its adherents. Shows how the movement forces personality distortion in many of its members.

Transcendental Meditation

Haddon, David, and Vail Hamilton. *TM Wants You! A Christian Response to Transcendental Meditation*. Grand Rapids: Baker, 1976. "Using a question and answer format, David Haddon clarifies the theology and philosophy undergirding TM and analyzes its claims—rest of body, tranquility of mind, increased mental ability, and personality development. Co-author Vail Hamilton shares her personal experiences as a former instructor of TM." One of the best Christian critiques of TM.

Weldon, John, and Zola Levitt. *The Transcendental Explosion*. Irvine, CA: Harvest House, 1976. A well-researched and extensively documented examination of TM by an expert in Eastern religions and the occult. Quoting practitioners and advocates as well as former practitioners and critics, the authors thoroughly critique the practices and underlying philosophy of TM. Includes four appendices dealing with TM's relationship to Hinduism, the occult, "serpent power," and reincarnation.

Unification Church

Elkins, Chris. *Heavenly Deception*. Wheaton, IL: Tyndale House, 1980. Tells the true story of the author's two-and-a-half year journey through the Unification Church and back to true faith in God. Gives information about the teachings and practices of the cult that is all the more persuasive because told by a former insider.

Yamamoto, J. Isamu. *The Puppet Master: An Inquiry into Sun Myung Moon and the Unification Church*. Downers Grove, IL: InterVarsity Press, 1977. The author, a former researcher with the Spiritual Counterfeits Project, provides an in-depth look at this subtly influential and dangerous cult. He includes a brief history of the movement, a glimpse into the shadowy life of Rev. Moon, a description of the recruitment and conversion process, an explanation of the complex and confusing teachings of Moon's Divine Principle, and concludes with a Christian response and biblical critique. Highly recommended.

The Way International

MacCollam, Joel. *The Way of Victor Paul Wierwille.* Downers Grove, IL: InterVarsity Press, 1978. A brief booklet exposing the errors and deceptions of Wierwille and his cult. Included as a chapter in Enroth et al., *A Guide to Cults and New Religions.*

Williams, J. L. *Victor Paul Wierwille and The Way International.* Chicago: Moody Press, 1979. The only book-length treatment of the Way International. Fully details Wierwille's anti-biblical heresies and aberrations, especially his denial of the full deity of Christ.

The Word-Faith Movement
(aka Positive Confession and the Health and Wealth Gospel)

Ankerberg, John, and John Weldon. *The Facts on False Teaching in the Church: What You Need to Know.* Eugene, OR: Harvest House, 1988. A needed and cogent exposé of the aberrant teachings of this rapidly growing movement among pentecostals and charismatics. Included as a chapter in the authors' book, *Cult Watch.*

Barron, Bruce. *The Health and Wealth Gospel.* Downers Grove, IL: InterVarsity Press, 1987. Documented with 24 pages of endnotes, this book "probes the teaching of prominent preachers" of the so-called Word-Faith Movement, showing where this teaching seriously deviates from biblical truth.

Horton, Michael, ed. *The Agony of Deceit.* Chicago: Moody Press, 1990. With chapters by Walter Martin, R. C. Sproul, C. Everett Koop, Joel Nederhood, and others, this is "an indepth, carefully documented analysis of television evangelism," in particular, the versions of the gospel propounded by the "positive confession," "positive thinking," and "possibility thinking" teachers. With numerous direct quotes from a wide selection of these men, the authors reveal "a gross deficiency of [the movement's] doctrinal foundations. In short, heresy."

McConnell, D. R. *A Different Gospel*. Peabody, MA: Hendrickson Publishers, 1989. Perhaps the best current exposé of Word-Faith errors, this book "exposes the historical links between the Faith Movement's 'Father,' Kenneth Hagin, Sr., and E. W. Kenyon, the influential writer schooled in New Thought metaphysics." In five pages of parallel columns, McConnell demonstrates how Hagin plagiarized whole paragraphs from the writings of Kenyon. McConnell also offers a biblical analysis of the Faith Movement's false teachings on "revelation knowledge," the "born-again Jesus," faith, healing, and prosperity.

Parker, Larry, and Don Tanner. *We Let Our Son Die*. Eugene, OR: Harvest House, 1980. This is the story of one couple's determination to live by the teachings of the Word-Faith Movement in regard to their son's affliction with diabetes, and the tragic consequences of taking him off his essential insulin. Relates how, even after the boy's death, the Parkers continued to blindly believe in the eventual miracle of his resurrection. When no miracle came and the parents were charged with negligent homicide, they finally realized the error of their belief and its devastating effects in their family.

The Worldwide Church of God (Armstrongism)

Chambers, Roger R. *The Plain Truth About Armstrongism*. Grand Rapids: Baker, 1972, 1989. An informative summary of the major errors of the Worldwide Church of God. Especially useful for its refutation of the so-called "Anglo-Israelism" espoused by the late founder Herbert W. Armstrong, recently repudiated by the current church leadership, but still held by numerous other fringe churches.

Hopkins, Joseph. *The Armstrong Empire*. Grand Rapids: Eerdmans, 1974. The most comprehensive examination of this "multi-million dollar religious empire best known popularly for its radio broadcast, 'The World Tomorrow,' and its magazine *The Plain Truth*."

Martin, Walter. *Herbert W. Armstrong and the Worldwide Church of God*. Minneapolis: Bethany House, 1985.

INDEX

Index

Bhagwan-type leaders, 134
Bible, 11, 26, 41, 49, 63, 88, 119,
    133–34, 143, 148, 178, 192
    false analogy justified with, 111
    as sole authority, 188
    taken out of context, 69 See also
        Bible study; Gospels
Bible Speaks, The, See Greater Grace
    World Outreach
Bible study, 68
    myths on, 54–57, 177
Biblical Evangelist, 221
Bjornstad, James, 9
Blitz, The, See Great Commission
    International
Blood, Linda O., 239
Bloom, Allan, 106, 113, 151
Boa, Kenneth, 9
Bob Larson Ministries, 221
Boston Church of Christ, 14–16, 24,
    49, 50, 68, 155, 202
    described, 36–38
Bothered About Dungeons and
    Dragons, 221
Bowman, Robert M., Jr., 235
Brahman, 101
Brainwashing, 117, 162
Brandon, Nathaniel, 58
Braswell, George W., Jr., 231–32
Breese, Dave, 232
Brooke, Tal, 238
Buddhism, 23, 108, 161, 182
Buehrer, Eric, 100
Building Your Christian Defense
    System (curriculum), 92
Burnout, 55, 68, 146, 149
Busséll, Harold, 21, 44, 62, 133, 180,
    232

Caleb's daughter (Bible), 64
Campus Crusade for Christ, 39, 40,
    97
Canada, resources in, 228
Captain, Philip, 91
CARIS, See Christian Apologetics:
    Research and Information
    Service
Catholic Church, 50
Cayce, Edgar, 26
Celibacy, 202
Center for Early Adolescence, The,
    98
Chambers, Roger R., 245
Chandler, Russell, 236
Changing World of Mormonism, The
    (Tanner & Tanner), 236

Chaos of the Cults, The (Van
    Baalen), 9
Charismatic groups, 33, 39, 44, 49,
    70, 71, 161, 181–82
Charles (case history), 198
Chesterton, G. K., 9
Cheyenne Mesa, 221
Child abuse, 93
Children of Darkness (Gordon), 235
Children of God, 24, 46, 59
    reading material on, 235
Children of God, The: The Inside
    Story (Davis & Davis), 235
Chinese Communists, 185
Christ Family, The, 24
Christian Apologetics: Research and
    Information Service (CARIS),
    221
Christian fellowship, See Fellowship
Christianity Today magazine, 34
Christian Ministries International
    (CMI), 221
Christian Reflections , 114
Christian Research Institute (CRI),
    158, 222
Christian Science, 26, 134
Christian Way International, Inc.,
    222
Christie (case history), 122–23
Churches, 92, 131–40
    lack of ministries for former
        cultists in, 135
    lack of teaching on cults in, 134
    responsibility for teaching doctrine
        in, 139–40
    unhelpful pastors in, 132–34
Churches of Christ, 50
Churches That Abuse (Enroth), 132,
    242
Church of Armageddon, 24
Church of Bible Understanding, 24
Church of Jesus Christ of Latter-Day
    Saints, See Mormonism
Church of the Living Word, 24, 33
Church Universal and Triumphant,
    25, 59
Citizens for Excellence in Education,
    100, 104
Clark, John, 51
Closing of the American Mind, The
    (Bloom), 106, 113, 151
CMI, See Christian Ministries
    International
Coercive groups, 29
Colson, Charles, 136

247

Index

Index

Index

typcial examples of, 25–26
One Way Relationships — When You Love Them More Than They Love You (Ells), 119
Origins of Totalitarianism (Arendt), 117
Ortiz, Juan Carlos, 109
Ottenweiler, Bishop Albert, 39
Overcontrol, parental, 88–89
Overdependence, 48, 49
Overprotectiveness, parental, 87

Pacific Institute for Research and Evaluation, 98
Paganism, 25
Painted Black (Raschke), 240
Panic, avoiding of, 156, 162
Pantheism, 23
Parents, 87–96, 163–64, 185
  addictions of, 94–95
  discipline and, 93, 95–96
  encouraging healthy friendships and, 127–30
  learning styles respected by, 92
  moral training and, 95
  obedience overemphasized by, 90–91
  overcontrol by, 88–89
  overprotectiveness by, 87
  recovery and, 180–81, 204–6 *See also* Families
Parent's Handbook, A, 105
Parker, Larry, 245
Park View Christian Fellowship, 203
Parkview Community Church, 39–40
Passantino, Gretchen, 107, 109, 234, 240
Passantino, Robert, 107, 109, 234, 240
Past, reemergence of, 198–99
Pastors, 157, 158, 162
  recovery and, 180, 181, 192–93
  unhelpful, 132–34
Paul (Bible), 13, 63, 64, 66, 88, 144, 148, 195
Pentecostal churches, 67
People's Temple, 27, 73, 91 *See also* Jones, Jim; Jonestown
Personal Freedom Outreach, 159, 225
Personality, attempts to change, 50, 122–24
Personality testing, 99
Peter (Bible), 13, 64, 111, 201
Phillips, Phil, 240
Piece of the Blue Sky: Scientology, Dianetics, and L. Ron Hubbard Exposed (Atack), 240–41

Pinnock, Clark H., 9
Plain Truth About Armstrongism, The (Chambers), 245
"Poison of Subjectivism, The" (Lewis), 114
Police, 159
Pornography, 137, 151
Positive Action Center, 226
Positive Confession movement, 24, 144 *See also* Word-Faith Movement
Posse Comitatus, 26
Potter's House/Victory Chapel/Door, The, 35–36
Poverty, 138
Powers (Korem), 239
Powers, Robert L., 240
Prana, 101, 102
Prayer, 12, 68, 186
Presbyterian Church, 50
Prince, Derek, 24
Prison or Paradise? The New Religious Cults (Rudin & Rudin), 234
Probe Ministries International, 226
Pro Family Forum, 99
Project 2000, 100
Proliferation of cults, 27–28
Prophet, Elizabeth Clare, 25
Prosperity teaching, 144
Psychic/occult/astral groups, *See* Occult
Psychological problems, myths on, *See under* Myths
Psychosis, 48, 52
Psychospiritual/self improvement groups, 24, 29
  typical examples of, 24–25
Puppet Master, The: An Inquiry into Sun Myung Moon and the Unification Church (Yamamoto), 243–44
Purity, demand for, 187
Purpose, regaining of, 191–92

Quest, 98–99
Questions
  asking of, 73–76
  discouragement of, 62–63

Raising PG Kids in an X-Rated Society (Gore), 239
Randy (case history), 53
Raschke, Carl A., 226, 240
Rawlings, Maurice S., 237–38
Reality testing, 196–97
Reason, experience vs., 71–72

Index